Making Money with
Multimedia

David Rosen and Caryn Mladen

Sponsored by Apple Computer, Inc.
Multimedia Development Group, New Media Division
for the Apple Multimedia Program

Addison-Wesley Publishers Ltd.
Don Mills, Ontario Reading, Massachusetts Menlo Park, California
New York Wokingham, England Amsterdam Bonn
Sydney Singapore Tokyo Madrid San Juan

Canadian Cataloguing in Publication Data

Rosen, David, 1961 -
Making Money with Multimedia
Includes bibliographical references and index.
ISBN 0-201-82283-0
1. CD-ROM. 2. CD-ROM industry. 3. New business enterprises. I. Mladen, Caryn, 1965 - II Title.
HD9696.0672R6 1994   338.7'6213976   C94-931847-7

Apple Direction Eileen LaPorte and Dana De Puy Morgan
Managing Editor Heather Rignanesi
Editor Mei Lin Cheung
Jacket Design Patty Richmond
Text Design Wycliffe Smith Design
Author Photographs Yasser Haidar

Acknowledgments

Hundreds of people have provided assistance in the writing of this book. The authors particularly thank the following:

- Arne Anderson
- Lesley Anne
- Wayne Arcus
- Gord Astles
- Marvin Avilez
- Lawrence Bekich
- Joseph Bogacz
- Brock Bohonos
- Beth Bruder
- Bridget Burke
- Satjiv Chahil
- Mei Lin Cheung
- John "Bud" Colligan
- Francisco d'Anconia
- Brian Davidson
- Dana De Puy Morgan
- Jane Dragone
- Barbara M. Drazga
- Kevin Fallon
- Joe Fantuzzi
- Leslie Fithian
- Steve Franseze
- Alisha Goh
- Herb Goodrich
- Yasser Haidar
- Stanley Halbreich
- Herbie Hancock
- Beatrice Harris
- Nicholas Henstock
- Isabel Hoffmann
- David Hudon
- Kent Johnson
- Peggy Kilburn
- Mark Langton
- Eileen LaPorte
- Ted Leonsis
- Wayne MacPhail
- Pat Maloney
- Nancy McCallister
- Cheri McCloskey
- Cameron McDonald-Stuart
- Lani Mercuro
- Austin Miller
- Michael Minnigan
- Mary Mladen
- Tom Mladen
- Katie Morgan
- Teri Nelson
- Jay Nobel
- Scott Olson
- Charles Paikert
- Phil Palmintere
- Jim Paxon
- George Perdicaris
- Janet Pivnick
- Brian Porter
- John Propper
- Patty Richmond
- Heather Rignanesi
- Burton Robson
- Iris Rosen
- Mary Rosen
- Julie Rusciolelli
- Andrew Scoular
- Kanwal Sharma
- Catherine Silver
- Paulette Siclari-Lee
- Steve Skelpewich
- Kim Slaton
- Lisa Sorge
- Rhonda Stratton
- Linda Shiozaki
- Gary Smith
- Willson Southam
- Joanna Tamer
- Glenn Tsunekawa
- Vicki Vance
- Richard Wah Kan
- Steve Wallace
- Ilbert Walker
- Jan Williams
- Paul Wollaston
- Gary Yentin
- Sarah Young
- Sara Zhanal
- Lynn Zucker
- Brad Zumwalt

©1994, David Rosen and Caryn Mladen. All rights reserved.

No part of this publication may be reproduced, stored in a retrieval system, or transmitted, in any form or by any means, mechanical, electronic, photocopying, recording or technology or system, known now or in future, without prior written permission of the authors. Printed in Canada. Mention of third party companis and products is for informational purposes only and constitutes neither an endorsement nor a recommendation.

APPLE LOGO, APPLELINK, HYPERCARD, AND MACINTOSH ARE TRADEMARKS OF APPLE COMPUTER, INC. REGISTERED IN THE UNITED STATES AND OTHER COUNTRIES.

QUICKTIME, SYSTEM 7, AND APPLE PROFESSIONAL VIDEO PRODUCTION SOLUTION ARE TRADEMARKS OF APPLE COMPUTER, INC.

A Hard Day's Night © 1964 Proscenium Films. A Hard Day's Night script © 1964 Proscenium Films. Software design © The Voyager Company.

ABC is a registered trademark of the American Broadcasting Corporation.

Adobe Illustrator and PostScript are trademarks of Adobe Systems Incorporated, which may be registered in certain jurisdictions.

America Online is a service mark of Quantum Computer Services, Inc.

Atari and Pong are registered trademarks of Atari Corporation.

AutoCAD is a registered trademark of Autodesk, Inc.

Brøderbund is a registered trademark of Brøderbund Software, Inc.

CD-I is a trademark of Philips and Sony.

Coke and Coca-Cola are registered trademarks of the Coca-Cola Company.

Compton's is a registered trademark of Compton's Learning Company.

CompuServe is a registered trademark of CompuServe Incorporated.

Discis Books is a registered trademark of Discis Knowledge Research Inc.

FileMaker Pro and MacWrite Pro are trademarks of Claris Corporation, registered in the United States of America and other countries.

IBM is a registered trademark of International Business Machines Corporation.

Intel is a registered trademark of Intel Corporation.

Internet is a trademark of Digital Equipment Corporation.

Kodak and PhotoCD are trademarks of Eastman Kodak Company.

LaserDisc and Pioneer are trademarks of Pioneer Electronic Corporation.

Lotus 1-2-3 is a registered trademark of Lotus Development Corporation.

Macromedia and SoundEdit Pro are trademarks and Authorware and Macromedia Director are registered trademarks of Macromedia, Inc.

Microsoft and Microsoft Word are registered trademarks and Windows is a trademark of Microsoft Corporation of Microsoft Corporation.

Nintendo Entertainment System (NES) and Super Mario Brothers are registered trademarks of Nintendo of America Inc.

Olympics is a registered trademark of the International Olympic Committee.

Pepsi is a registered trademark of Pepsico.

RasterOps is a registered trademark of RasterOps Corp.

Sega and Sonic the Hedgehog are registered trademarks of Sega Corporation.

Sony and Sony Electronic Publishing are registered trademarks of Sony Corporation.

The Voyager Company and The Expanded Book Toolkit are trademarks of The Voyager Company.

XPLORA 1 is a registered trademark of Real World Studios.

Mention of third party companies and products is for informational purposes only and constitutes neither an endorsement or a recommendation. Apple, Addison-Wesley, David Rosen, Caryn Mladen, their respective agents or assigns assume no responsibility with regard to the selection, performance, or use of any products, services, techniques or strategies outlined in this book. All understandings, agreements, or warranties, if any, take place between the vendors and the prospective users. Please note that these products and services have not been tested by Apple, Addison-Wesley, David Rosen or Caryn Mladen and the material herein does not represent a complete summary of the information available.

EVEN THOUGH APPLE, ADDISON-WESLEY, DAVID ROSEN OR CARYN MLADEN HAVE REVIEWED THIS MATERIAL, APPLE, ADDISON-WESLEY, DAVID ROSEN OR CARYN MLADEN MAKE NO WARRANTY OR REPRESENTATION, EITHER EXPRESS OR IMPLIED, WITH RESPECT TO THIS BOOK, ITS QUALITY, ACCURACY, MERCHANTABILITY, OR FITNESS FOR A PARTICULAR PURPOSE. AS A RESULT, THIS MATERIAL IS DISTRIBUTED "AS IS," AND YOU, THE RECIPIENT, ARE ASSUMING THE ENTIRE RISK AS TO ITS QUALITY AND ACCURACY.

IN NO EVENT WILL APPLE COMPUTER, INC., ADDISON-WESLEY PUBLISHERS LIMITED, DAVID ROSEN OR CARYN MLADEN BE LIABLE FOR DIRECT, INDIRECT, SPECIAL, INCIDENTAL, OR CONSEQUENTIAL DAMAGES RESULTING FROM ANY DEFECT OR INACCURACY IN THIS BOOK, EVEN IF ADVISED OF THE POSSIBILITY OF SUCH DAMAGES.

The warranty and remedies set forth above are exclusive and in lieu of all other, oral or written, express or implied. No Apple or Addison-Wesley dealer, agent, or employee or David Rosen or Caryn Mladen is authorized to make any modification, extension, or addition to this warranty. Some jurisdictions do not allow the exclusion or limitation of implied warranties or liabilities for incidental or consequential damages, so the above limitation or exclusion may not apply to you. This warranty gives you specific legal rights, and you may also have other rights that vary from jurisdiction to jurisdiction.

Welcome to *Making Money with Multimedia!*

Multimedia is a burgeoning marketplace. According to industry experts, the multimedia market is expected to be a $24-billion industry by the year 2000. To be successful in multimedia you have to know the industry, the market, and your competitors. Technical knowledge is not enough.

Apple is committed to the growth and success of multimedia and its pioneers. *Making Money with Multimedia* — sponsored by the Apple Multimedia Program — is an example of Apple's commitment to provide resources for developing, marketing, and distributing successful multimedia products.

Making Money with Multimedia is written for anyone who wants to succeed in multimedia. Whether you are a current or potential commercial or in-house corporate developer, investor, venture capitalist, or merely interested in keeping up-to-date, *Making Money with Multimedia* will help you make multimedia your competitive advantage.

Making Money with Multimedia is a business book focusing on financing, marketing, sales, and financial planning for multimedia projects and services. In clear, easy-to-understand language, this book will help you finance, manage, and profitably distribute your multimedia product or service — on time and on budget.

Read on and explore!

Satjiv S. Chahil
Vice President and General Manager
New Media Division
Apple Computer, Inc.

CONTENTS

Introduction We Know Who You Are — 1
The Book – *Making Money with Multimedia* — 2
Multimedia Developers and Programmers — 2
Who Else Can Benefit? — 3
Why Technical Knowledge Is not Enough — 3
Summing Up — 3

Chapter 1 The Multimedia Food Chain – Where YOU Fit In — 5
Models – How Your Business Operates — 6
The Multimedia Food Chain — 8

Chapter 2 Types of Multimedia Projects — 18
CD-ROM Titles — 18
Kiosks — 20
Business Presentations — 21
Multimedia Databases — 22
Corporate Training — 24
Key Examples of Multimedia That Sell — 24

Chapter 3 Business Planning — 30
General Overview of the Business Plan — 31
Why You Need a Business Plan — 31
Performance and Viability — 32
Structure of the Business Plan — 35
How Multimedia Business Plans Differ from Traditional Business Plans — 42
How to Find People to Fill in the Gaps in Your Skill Set — 43

Chapter 4 Marketing 101 — 44
What Marketing Means — 44
Using the Business Plan — 45
Advertising — 46
How Marketing Equals Leverage — 47
Product Marketing — 53
Solutions Marketing — 54
Press Relations — 55

Chapter 5 Introduction to Sales — 56
Selling Multimedia — 56
Selling Multimedia Services — 58
Sales Levels — 58
How to Find Prospects — 60
Preparation and Presentation — 61
Service After the Sale — 62
Getting Paid — 63

Chapter 6 Introduction to Finance — 64
The Importance of Finance — 64
The Income Statement — 66
The Balance Sheet — 69
The Statement of Retained Earnings — 71
The Statement of Changes in Financial Position — 72
Reading Financial Statements — 73
Depreciation — 77
Taxes, Permits, and Licensing — 78
How to Talk with Your Banker or Venture Capitalist — 78

Chapter 7 Distribution – How to Get Your Product to Your Customers — 80
Introduction to Distribution — 80
Three Publishing Options — 82
Costs of Distribution — 85
Fulfillment Companies — 90
Understanding North American Distribution Realities — 91
What Distributors Look for in a New Product — 93
Bundling — 96

Chapter 8 How to Determine Your First Title or Project — 100
Look at the Market and See What's Needed — 100
In-House Intrigue — 101
Tips on How to Attract a Producer — 103
Finding Your Niche — 104

Chapter 9 Solutions Marketing in the Education World — 108
Multimedia in Today's Schools — 108
Marketing Multimedia to Schools — 110
Targeting the Decision-Makers — 111
Where to Sell? — 113
Trends in K—12 Education — 116
New Media Centers — 119
Trends in Higher Education — 120

Chapter 10 Solutions Marketing in the Business World — 121
Archiving — 121
General Communications — 122
Collaborative Work — 123
Business Presentations — 124
Corporate Education and Training — 126
Understanding the Players in a Large Corporation — 127
Understanding the Sales Cycle in a Large Corporation — 129
Working with a Non-Technical Business or Entrepreneur — 130
What Businesses Look for in a Multimedia Vendor — 130
What Types of Businesses Are the Best Targets for Your Projects — 131
What Projects Have the Best Chance of Success — 132

Chapter 11 Solutions Marketing in the Consumer and Home Markets — 134
The Potential Market for Consumer Titles and Content — 134
How to Sell to the Consumer Market — 135
Meet the Giants of Consumer Publishing and Distribution — 136
Focusing on CD-ROM Title Subjects — 141

Chapter 12 Press Relations – Why You Need It! — 145
Meet the Players — 145
Understanding Press Relations — 147
Press Kits with One-Offs — 149
Customizing Your Marketing Material for the Press — 151
PR Firms — 151
Trade Shows and Promotions — 152
Making Press Relations Equal Sales — 154

Chapter 13 Summing Up — 155
The Basics — 156
Plan Ahead — 157
How to Read the Market and Read about the Market — 158
The Future for Multimedia — 158

Chapter 14 Sample Documents — 159
News Release — 160
Business Plan — 161

Chapter 15 Sources — 169

Index — 210

Introduction
We Know Who You Are

You're standing in a bookstore thinking about your future, wondering if this book is for you. You are interested in multimedia and want to find out how to take the next step – creating your own project. You're keeping up to date in the ever-expanding multimedia industry. Perhaps you're a content developer trying to figure out how to create, package, and deliver your product. You want to invest your money, time, and talent in a multimedia project and need to know what your next steps should be. You may come from the computer, entertainment, or financial industries, or you have a great idea for an original product that only multimedia will bring to life.

You've picked up this book at the right time. According to industry experts, the multimedia market is expected to be a $24-billion industry by the year 2000. But nobody's waiting around for it to happen by itself. Already, people are scrambling to stake out their claim in the burgeoning multimedia marketplace. Freeman Associates – an industry research company based in California – estimates that worldwide installed base of CD-ROM drives will pass the 42-million mark by 1995. With that large a market, a variety of competitive players has arrived on the scene. If you are going to be successful, you must know how to deal with your market, your competitors, and the industry heavyweights.

The Book –
Making Money with Multimedia

We wrote this book with three main groups in mind. First, *Making Money with Multimedia* helps current and potential software developers understand the business side of multimedia. Second, the book helps in-house corporate developers and computer people to plan and develop multimedia projects. Finally, *Making Money with Multimedia* provides a cookbook for people on the business side of multimedia. "People on the business side" refer to investors, venture capitalists, computer vendors, managers, entrepreneurs, and the like. In short, we mean anyone who needs to understand the business concerns unique to multimedia development. Business people need to understand how multimedia can add profit to an organization's bottom line. *Making Money with Multimedia* helps you make informed decisions about multimedia projects and how to use multimedia as your competitive advantage in the marketplace.

Multimedia Developers and Programmers

The multimedia market is characterized by thousands of small start-up companies and not by industry giants like Microsoft, Lotus, and Computer Associates. Unfortunately, few of the people operating these start-ups have formal training or useful experience in the business of multimedia. This book explains key business concepts to anyone who wants to succeed in the multimedia industry. Using simple language, this book can help you create, manage, and profitably distribute your multimedia project – on time and on budget.

Who Else Can Benefit?

Many in-house corporate information systems professionals are responsible for creating and producing multimedia projects. Other in-house people are responsible for **outsourcing** multimedia projects to third-party companies. These people need to be able to judge if a particular multimedia production company will be in business by the end of the project. If you are part of this group, *Making Money with Multimedia* will benefit you because it provides an accurate way to cost, charge back, and distribute in-house multimedia projects. Sections covering business planning, obtaining financing, and copyright and trademark issues are included in this book.

OUTSOURCING
The process by which key functions of a company (data processing, for example) are contracted out to unrelated firms to save money or improve efficiency.

Why Technical Knowledge Is not Enough

More often than not technical ability is just the first step in having a successful software product. Many technical folks spend years slaving over the proverbial hot keyboard cooking up the next masterpiece only to find no market, no sales, no profits, and no future. If only they had spent a small portion of their development time researching the marketing and sales aspects of their product! By the time you've read this book you will have a good understanding of what steps are involved in making money with multimedia, or any software application for that matter.

Summing Up

Making Money with Multimedia is unique in that it explains the business side of development – the multimedia food chain, business planning, multimedia marketing, distribution models, solutions sales, press relations, and much more.

Chapter 1

The Multimedia Food Chain— where YOU fit in

Have you ever wondered what it takes to become a multimedia title developer? More to the point, have *you* ever wondered if *you* have what it takes? Can *you* become the first multimedia Scorsese, Coppola, or Spielberg? This chapter outlines the important roles necessary for an average multimedia project and explains what each person must do to make the project successful. If you're already familiar with multimedia production, this chapter can be used as a checklist. If you're just starting out on the long road to multimedia development, the following information will probably save you time, money, and aggravation.

Developing a multimedia project is something like performing a plate spinning act from the old Ed Sullivan show. As soon as you get everything spinning, you have to go back to the beginning to make sure nothing falls and shatters. Of course, keeping all those plates spinning is much easier when you spin them right the first time, *and* when you have a few trusted and experienced professionals on stage with you. This is what multimedia development is all about: having good ideas implemented by the right professionals all of whom have strong **skill sets**.

This does not mean you can't do it all yourself. Many developers have started projects in their basements but this may prove too great a hassle in the long run. Most multimedia projects require more and different skills than do traditional programming jobs.

SKILL SETS
The talents, professional capabilities, and technical know how that allow a multimedia professional to get the job done properly.

Depending on your project, multimedia development may require skills such as video editing, animation, and story writing. It will definitely require careful planning and marketing skills. It is rare to find one individual capable of all necessary tasks. Besides, doing everything yourself isn't much fun. And multimedia is supposed to be fun, isn't it?

Multimedia has developed from a convergence of many industries, most notably the entertainment, film, and computer industries. As movie producers say, "It's not called show *business* for nothing." A movie won't get made unless someone (usually a producer) is convinced that the project is financially viable and potentially profitable. The same is true for a multimedia project. Okay, so the average multimedia project may not require millions of dollars, hundreds of technical professionals, blockbuster stars, and a year or so of production time. Still, multimedia projects *do* involve a fair bit of money, technical professionals, interesting content, and detailed production work. Considering the scope of many titles released in the last few years, the trend is for higher production values and well-known content. You will probably have to start using those expensive Hollywood touches on your project just to be competitive.

Models – How Your Business Operates

Before we get started on the who's who of multimedia we have to understand where everybody fits into the big picture. Multimedia businesses usually operate on one of three main business models. These are the publishing model, the movie model, and the software maintenance model. Other models include the video game model, the home video rental model, and the music industry model.

Popularized by the traditional book publishing industry, you would probably use the publishing model if you are working on a small electronic book or magazine. This model would also be useful if, for example, you are taking existing content, adding **interactivity** and then publishing it onto a CD-ROM. Using the

INTERACTIVITY
The capability for two-way communication and interaction between the computer and the user.

publishing model, a core group of individuals organizes independent contractors for the artistic and technical requirements of the project. Not infrequently the director acts as the producer, the project manager and, possibly, even the sales and marketing manager. Since everyone on the project is doubling up, jobs are typically filled by people with generalized content knowledge. These people may lack the specific skills necessary to make the project a blockbuster hit. Sometimes a publisher will commission a developer (or author) to create a specific work, while in other circumstances authors approach publishers to get their work published. In both cases, most of the production work is done in-house.

The movie model involves a central group of business professionals, usually a producer, a team of lawyers, and a few financial and marketing people. These professionals outsource and assemble a group of artistic specialists capable of undertaking the multimedia project. Many large multimedia production companies operate with this model because these organizations are typically working on more than one project at a time. In this model, separate production groups are responsible for the external production of particular assignments. Upper management is responsible for financing, budgeting, and general organization. This model features a minimum of coordination between the separate groups.

The third model used in multimedia development is that of the software maintenance model. This model is used in multimedia development for an on-going project likely to require after-sales support, or a project with a constantly changing user base or content that is continually changing or evolving. Examples of such projects are in-house computer-based training (CBT) projects and the development of multimedia programming tools themselves.

Business models help establish relationships, responsibilities, and reporting structures between staff members. No matter which business model you use to run your project, pick the one that works best for you and your situation.

The Multimedia Food Chain

To get a good idea of the players involved in a typical multimedia project take a look at the Multimedia Food Chain below.

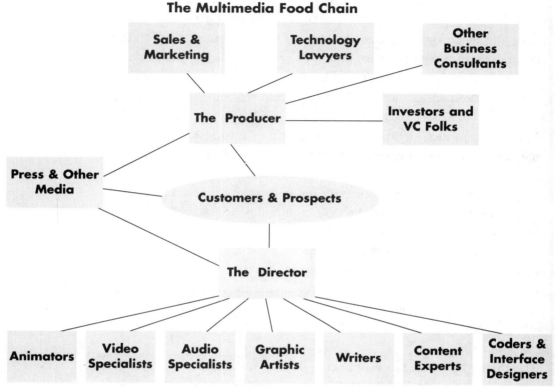

This group is sometimes known as "The Talent."

Not every potential role is illustrated – nor will every project need someone in every position. It is, however, a good road map for figuring out how *your* skills and the skills of your associates fit into the typical requirements of a multimedia project. Now that we understand the big picture, let's concentrate on some of the players and the skills each needs to be successful in your organization. We'll start with the business side of the Multimedia Food Chain.

Multimedia developers can get valuable information and support from developer assistance programs, such as the Apple Multimedia Program. Refer to Chapter 15, page 202, for details.

The Producer –
The Project Boss

Being a multimedia producer means you have the final say on the business side of the project. Remember those spinning plates we talked about earlier? It's the producer's job to keep those plates spinning at all times. The producer's project management skills are extremely important since it usually falls on the producer's shoulders to manage the entire project (although sometimes this responsibility is shared with the director). Project management means making realistic deadlines and budgets, and sticking to them. If a producer is not administratively inclined, a detail-oriented administrative assistant should be hired.

A SUCCESSFUL PRODUCER HAS —
- *original idea*
- *organizational skills*
- *access to $$$*
- *experience in subject matter*
- *understanding of and experience with multimedia projects*

One of the most important roles for any producer is figuring out how to get enough money into the company to fund the project. As producer, you arrange for the initial financing to bankroll the project and you keep a sharp eye on all the financial details. If the company has established a track record, producers can sometimes deal with bankers for debt financing or venture capitalists (VC) for **equity financing** (also called investment). In most cases, however, you have to be generating over a million dollars in sales before either group will listen to you. If neither bank nor VC funding is available, producers have to reach into their own pockets. Having said that, you may be able to get financing if your project looks good enough, and if you have already got the contracts for content and distribution in your pocket. By looking good, we mean that you have an impressive business plan and interesting initial demos or prototypes. If you're developing your first title, you probably won't get financing without *all* these elements.

EQUITY FINANCING

Getting money into the company by selling off a percentage of the company to an investor or venture capitalist. This investor or venture capitalist then becomes a joint owner in your company proportional to his or her investment.

Producers also have to worry about the legal issues of the project. From copyright infringement to trademark problems, from piracy to privacy, legal issues can stall and sometimes even kill your project completely. It's the producer's job to work with a technology lawyer to keep the project safe. Finally, the producer has to be concerned with signing up business. Sales and marketing *should* be two of the primary concerns when one starts to think about multimedia development. Unfortunately, they are often the last. The producer should follow a good business plan that sets out the objectives, strategies, and tactics involved in moving a multimedia company from today to a profitable tomorrow.

Sales and Marketing Consultants –
The Spin Doctors Who Create the Demand

Believe it or not, many developers spend all their time and money creating a particular multimedia piece with no thought as to how the eventual project will be sold. Only after they've invested hundreds or thousands of hours of work do they start thinking about actually selling the project.

A successful sales and marketing consultant has —
- *understanding of multimedia industry*
- *experience in computer or technology sales*
- *contacts in the industry*
- *people skills*
- *understanding of channel distribution*

Do movie producers spend millions of dollars making feature films without considering who will pay to watch them? Of course not. However, many multimedia developers mistakenly believe that a market will somehow develop, promotional material will design and produce itself, sales channels will be constructed, and product demand will magically self-generate. In fact, marketing and demand generation activities should be planned from the start. Unless you have considerable marketing experience in the computer, publishing, or movie-making sectors (depending on your content and audience), you should consider hiring a marketing consultant to help you keep on track. Several market research companies have exceptionally detailed forecast reports that can help you determine where to target your marketing.

Selected market research companies are listed in Chapter 15 under "Sources."

Technology Lawyer –
WHAT YOU DON'T KNOW CAN HURT YOU

Television courtroom drama is fun to watch. However, it loses its appeal when it's you sitting in the witness box defending yourself in a trademark or copyright suit. Legislation has most certainly not kept pace with the times and this leads to all sorts of potential problems for multimedia development. Technology law is at best murky. It's necessary to consult a technology lawyer to protect yourself in the multimedia world.

A GOOD TECHNOLOGY LAWYER HAS –
- *sound background knowledge of intellectual property*
- *negotiating ability*
- *solid understanding of your technology*

INVESTORS AND VENTURE CAPITALISTS –
THE FOLKS WHO MAKE THE GOLDEN RULES

Multimedia projects can be extremely expensive, and most developers cannot foot the bill alone. A few graphics or video clips can cost thousands of dollars and require hundreds of hours of production time. Investors and venture capitalists provide the money or the **financing leverage** to get the project done. They don't do this for free, so don't expect someone to fall in love with your project and just give you all the money you need. You will have to give up a percentage of the profits or a part of the business, and sometimes you will have to give up a controlling share. A developer has to prove to an investor that the project will make more money than it costs – in fact, a *lot* more money. Investors are looking not only for a great return on their investment, but also a timely return, and a good chance that the project will not fail. Remember, investors call the shots. They can put their money into your project or any one of a thousand other ventures. If it's your first or second project, you probably need them more than they need you, so give them a well thought-out and properly researched business plan. Give them periodic reports. Wise investors will need to know how you are going to spend the investment money. Don't give them any reason for pulling out of the project.

A SUCCESSFUL INVESTOR OR VENTURE CAPITALIST HAS –
- *money*
- *industry contacts*
- *connections with underwriters*
- *experience in high-tech industry*

FINANCING LEVERAGE
The ability to control a company or project with a minimal amount of cash.

That being said, we've seen cases where investors have hindered the project through excessive baby-sitting. The producer needs to spend time dealing with the project, not with the investor. If an investor has contacts or channels for marketing or distribution, these should be shared with the producer. If the investor does not believe the producer is competent, the investment should not have been made in the first place. If the producer is competent, he or she should be left to do the job.

PRESS AND MEDIA RELATIONS –
MAKING YOU A STAR

Print journalists as well as television and radio personalities often have the power to make or break your multimedia project. The savvy producer or marketing professional will actively seek out these influencers as an important step in making sales. If you have a CD-ROM game or other retail product, a good press write-up can make your company into an overnight sensation. Even in-house work can benefit from media attention. Many in-house multimedia producers have been catapulted into the executive limelight by favorable mention of a project in the trade press or even the company newsletter. An aggressive PR effort can bring invaluable visibility to your product.

A GOOD PRESS AND MEDIA RELATIONS EXPERT HAS —
- *good writing and communication skills*
- *people skills*
- *contacts with press and media*
- *educational background in technology and marketing*

The Director –
Heads up the Talent

A multimedia director has artistic control over the final product and is therefore often called "Creative Director." He or she is the liaison between the business side (the producer and investors) and the artistic side (the animators, videographers, and so on). Sometimes the role of the director is played by the producer, especially in relatively low budget productions. Project management skills are vital for successful directors who have to keep the content and technology plates spinning, and often act as writer or designer of the overall project. Directors often have to source out or hire on contract the technical and artistic professionals to make the project work. Directors rely on their contacts in the industry for their staffing needs. Temperamental stars exist beyond the land of feature films, and a successful director must be able to control big creative egos.

> **A successful director has –**
> - *experience in entertainment industry*
> - *project management skills*
> - *leadership abilities*
> - *understanding of the technology and of the talent*
> - *artistic background or experience*

The Talent
Animators –
Bringing Line Drawing to Life

Depending on the nature of your project, animators can add a special flair to your content. Animation also makes watching and interacting with your presentation or disc more exciting. Traditional animators use paper and ink sketches, which are then digitized into a computer with the help of a scanner. These images are usually cleaned up with the help of an editing package and then placed into an animation package for further work. Many younger animators avoid the paper-and-ink method and prefer to draw directly on the computer with a mouse or pressure sensitive tablet. Cities like New York, Los Angeles, Chicago, San Francisco, Bangalore, London, Toronto, Sydney, Vancouver,

> **A good animator has –**
> - *talent at drawing animations and rendering*
> - *wide range of styles*
> - *ability to create animations for specific purposes*
> - *ability to storyboard*
> - *ability to keep deadlines*

Hong Kong, and Singapore all have thriving animation communities. Most universities and colleges have small animation programs creating pockets of newly minted animators. However, don't confuse education with ability. Just because someone has an impressive degree doesn't mean he or she can create the effects you want.

Video Specialists –
Lights, Camera, Action!

Videographers who can handle camera, lights, and even the sound for an on-location shoot are plentiful, especially in major cities. Choose videographers by looking at their portfolio footage and finding out if they have any experience in digitization, compression, and sound synchronization. Ask detailed questions about how they achieve their effects to ensure they really know what they are talking about.

A GOOD VIDEO SPECIALIST HAS —
- *ability to edit video*
- *skill in the use of video equipment*
- *experience in audio/video synchronization*

Audio Specialists –
Shout Your Message

Almost all multimedia projects use sound to communicate. How do you get your desired audio (voice narration and special effects) into the computer? There are two ways: record it yourself or reuse existing audio. We recommend using a professional studio and experts in audio for projects aimed at public distribution. If you record it in-house, you should know there's more to recording and playing back sound than just using the microphone attached to your computer. In sound recording (as with all aspects of multimedia production work), you should consider the expectations of your audience. For all but the most forgiving audiences (like viewers of low end in-house or rough storyboarding work), you'll need to use a professional recording studio.

A GOOD AUDIO SPECIALIST HAS —
- *ability to edit audio*
- *ability to produce clear sounds*
- *ability to produce a wide range of sounds*
- *extensive understanding of audio equipment*
- *experience in audio/video synchronization*

If you choose to reuse existing audio by licensing the track from someone else, be sure to consult your lawyer to secure the appropriate rights.

Content Experts –
PERFECTING THE SUBJECT MATTER

Depending on the complexity of the project – and other factors including financing and legal concerns – the role of the content expert may be filled by the director or an industry specialist. Content experts research your subject matter and ensure that the quality of your material is consistently excellent. Content experts understand the content *thoroughly* and know what the intended audience needs to be told about the subject matter. The best way to find knowledgeable content experts is to look through the pages of trade publications or to cull names from trade show speaker lists.

A GOOD CONTENT EXPERT HAS –
- *expertise and reputation in subject matter*
- *communication skills*
- *research skills*

Writers –
COMMUNICATING WITH THE AUDIENCE

These people are responsible for writing – and proofing – the actual text your customers will see on the screen and the words they will hear. Depending on your intended market, it may be advantageous for your writer to be able to speak other languages. In some cases, these professionals write the scripts for voice-overs and the audio associated with video clips. Writers and content experts work closely together to develop the flow of information.

A GOOD WRITER HAS –
- *writing talent*
- *experience in writing for multimedia projects*
- *ability to get the message across*
- *ability to meet deadlines*
- *proof-reading skills*

Graphic Designers, Artists, Illustrators, and Photographers –

The Artistic Touch

Good graphic designers, artists, illustrators, and photographers have —
- *talent and experience in particular fields*
- *familiarity with multimedia tools*
- *ability to receive and execute instructions*
- *creativity*

Graphic designers, illustrators, photographers, and image scanning and processing technicians are all artists. Directors know what style is important to the project and find the artist to create it. Some graphic artists have been classically trained in college or university while others have picked up their skills as they developed their craft. Determine the artistic and aesthetic quality and style of your candidates by examining examples of their completed work. It is important to ensure that the artists working on your project can create the image and overall look that you want. It's also a good idea to ensure that the artists can take instruction from the director. Spend some time getting to know their work habits and character. If you want your talent to work during the business day and they like to start work at seven o'clock in the evening, you may want to reconsider the situation.

The character and habits of everyone in the food chain should be considered right from the beginning.

Coders and Interface Designers –
PROVIDING A STRUCTURAL FRAMEWORK

Last, but certainly not least, are the coders and interface designers. These people usually have a formal programming or systems background. To them, multimedia development environments are simply another language in which to code and express ideas. Some colleges and university extension schools teach the skills needed to become a multimedia coder or interface designer. A few of these organizations have co-op programs in which students work in multimedia companies during or after their formal studies. During this time the students get paid by the school. Investigating these programs can result in a windfall of talent for your project. Pilot projects like the Apple New Media Centers hold promise to develop and encourage young talent.

A GOOD CODER AND INTERFACE DESIGNER HAS —
- *talent at fitting interface to project*
- *understanding of all inputs*
- *experience in multimedia coding or design*
- *background in graphic design*

The Apple New Media Centers are described in Chapter 9.

Chapter 2

Types of Multimedia Projects

In this chapter we are going to introduce some of the many ways using multimedia can put money in your pocket. By no means is this list exhaustive but it should get you thinking in the right direction.

CD-ROM Titles

The Compact Disc-Read Only Memory (CD-ROM) is the most popular and predominant tool for delivering multimedia these days. CD-ROMs are just like CD audio discs except that CD-ROMs tend to hold a lot more than just sound and music tracks. CD-ROMs are formatted differently as well. A CD-ROM can hold up to 650 Mb or more of information. To put this into perspective, a complete twenty-six volume encyclopedia, complete with text, graphics, sounds, animations, and even some full motion video clips can be stored on a single two-ounce CD-ROM disc.

The advantages of CD-ROM technology are numerous. These include high storage capacity at significantly lower cost. One CD-ROM disc can hold up to a 250,000 pages of text, 12,000 images, or over an hour of video and audio. Other key advantages are the low cost of the physical disc, low shipping costs associated with a light-weight product, the permanence of information storage, and the ease of cross-platform compatibility.

In the past, the problems with CD-ROMs were related to relatively slow data transfer rates and access times. As a result, for example, digital video could be jerky and lack synchronization, and could freeze while the computer gathered more information. These problems have been overcome with advances in hardware and software technology.

The current CD-ROM title market can be classified into three broad markets: education, entertainment, and business. In creating CD-ROM titles, your focus should be content and the market interested in that content. They say "Content is King" in the multimedia industry, and it's no joke. Whether you are repurposing previously created material or creating the material yourself, you must use material that people want. Otherwise, the greatest packaging and marketing program in the world will not sell your product. As we mentioned in the Introduction, the market for CD-ROMs is growing by leaps and bounds. According to Freeman Associates, the worldwide installed base of computer-based CD-ROM drives will rise to 60 million units in 1996 and grow to almost 80 million in 1997.

Many multimedia companies have made money **bundling** their CD-ROM discs with computer hardware. For example, a CD-ROM drive vendor pays the CD-ROM developer a small licensing fee per disc (usually between $1 and $3) for the right to reproduce and distribute the CD-ROM with his or her company's drives. Work the numbers. If the vendor sells 50,000 CD-ROM drives, you'll receive your licensing fee times 50,000. We'll be covering bundling opportunities for CD-ROMs in Chapter 7 but you should realize that this is a multimillion-dollar business involving the major hardware manufacturers, distributors, and content developers. Bundling is a good way to introduce your company name to the industry and to customers.

BUNDLING
The inclusion of your product (a CD-ROM, for example) with another vendor's hardware or software.

KIOSKS

Kiosks can either provide information or do transactions. Informational **kiosks** may provide directions, music clips, advertising, trade show opportunities, or tourism promotions. Transactional kiosks, on the other hand, allow you to get something or do something as a result of your query, such as **.i. station** music or movie rentals. Automatic teller machines at your bank, and insurance machines at the airport, are typical examples of transactional kiosks. Major corporations typically use kiosks to provide consistent, tireless access to information and other things like money for their customers. The downside is that kiosk information cannot be changed frequently because it is time-consuming and physically difficult. You must open up the kiosk enclosure, add the new information to the hard drive, and test it. All this takes place in a busy shopping mall or other high traffic area.

KIOSKS
Computer-based devices that allow information access or transactions. Typically kiosks are placed in shopping malls, airports, or other high traffic areas.

.i. station
An interactive kiosk designed by the in-touch group of San Francisco. This kiosk is found in selected music stores and lets you listen to your choice of music by artist, song, or subject.

To create an effective kiosk, you need to design an interactive project that does not require a keyboard and which may be used by people who don't know much about computers. When you design your interactive project, always keep in mind your target audience. There is a fine line between providing sufficient information to get the job done and excess information that will end up confusing kiosk users. Just about every kiosk you will come across operates using a touch screen so that customers merely need to touch a point on the screen to answer simple questions to get the job done.

Design your interface from the ground up to accept touch-screen input – make your text and buttons larger than you might otherwise.

Types of Multimedia Projects

If you design kiosks, you may end up reinventing the wheel. Kiosks are customized, and there is no central directory for you to search to find out if your project has been done before. Kiosks will typically be commissioned by a corporation. It is rare and very risky for a kiosk developer to think up an idea for a kiosk, create it, and then go searching for a market. Making a kiosk is expensive because it is customized to the particular task, content, and company. Recently, multimedia companies have started to standardize key elements to make kiosk creation a more cost-effective venture. If you have been commissioned to create a kiosk, listen hard to what your corporate contacts request. They will likely have a corporate vision they want you to implement. Ask questions, get particulars. You can certainly make suggestions, but be clear about your costs and capabilities. Otherwise you will set yourself up to disappoint your clients.

The sales aspects of multimedia kiosks are covered in Chapter 5.

Business Presentations

Some multimedia businesses are based on creating sales presentations and presentation software in digital form and delivered on CD-ROM. These presentations can, for example, incorporate digitized movies, sound for playback, and near VHS quality video from a CD-ROM drive. If you need quality broadcast playback, traditional magnetic hard drives rather than CD-ROM drives should be used. The performance and capacity of CD-ROM drives are constantly improving, as are compression techniques, but still lag behind hard drive playback capabilities. Business presentations based on CD-ROMs are expected to increase in popularity and prominence.

Multimedia Databases

A specialized usage for multimedia can be found in multimedia databases. Multimedia databases or catalogs are likely to be profitable as business-based applications. This is because the research and preparation required to create a complete database on any subject are extremely expensive. Also the market for particular types of information in a multimedia format may be limited. These databases can be contained on a CD-ROM, in a kiosk, or can be accessed over the Internet or other on-line services. The heart of any multimedia presentation is its ability to communicate thoughts, ideas, and emotions. The real value of multimedia in a database is its ability to hold the attention of the viewer and possibly sell something.

INTERNET
A loose affiliation of computer-based database and information access points spread throughout the world.

Multimedia databases are not merely text-based information that have been transferred onto a CD-ROM disc. Telephone books are now available on CD-ROM but they are not multimedia databases even though they allow you to search by name, address, telephone number, or any other included data. To be true multimedia tools they must include more than just text. They must also include at least one of the following: audio, video, animations, graphics, or photographs. Telephone directories can't act as multimedia marketing tools without at least one of these elements.

However, product catalogs *can* act as excellent multimedia marketing tools. *En Passant* – a CD-ROM-based home shopping trial – is an example of interactive catalogs. With *En Passant*, you can select products from any of 21 different on-line catalogs. Each product comes complete with a picture on movie, bringing customers right into the new "store." You can distribute sales information, infomercials, or direct marketing on a single CD-ROM disc. The major problem in the past with this marketing technique is that relatively few computer owners had CD-ROM drives. But, as we mentioned earlier in this chapter, this is changing.

Increasingly, CD-ROM drives will find their way into the home market to satisfy the demand for games (with the likes of Sega, Nintendo, and even 3DO). Macintosh and Intel-based computers will also account for significant market growth. Catalogs on CD-ROM promise to become a successful marketing tool in the future.

Interactive shopping discs can help people overcome an inherent reluctance to use technology. In the *En Passant* trial, for example, each customer who responded to the survey reported that he or she used the disc for over four hours total and then passed it on to a family member or friend.

Using humor is a great way to achieve these goals. A kiosk in a mall can appear to contain a man trapped within the kiosk, begging all passers-by to push the red button or to touch a particular part of the touch-screen. His antics are likely to interest shoppers who will perform this simple function for him. They will then get equally simple instructions to continue to use the database. Presto! The database is being accessed.

Typical applications of this technology are in real estate, travel and tourism businesses, or in other businesses that want to sell high market items. They need new ways to interest their market, and multimedia databases can do the job. If you want to get involved with multimedia databases, remember that you might be presenting an enhanced sales pitch for your client. So only attempt this kind of multimedia if you have talent or support in marketing and sales. Have a look at other multimedia-enabled databases. *We Make Memories, Share with Me a Story*, and *Voices of the 30s* all provide in-depth interactive information without giving the feeling that you are accessing a database.

Corporate Training

Like the business presentation market, making money in corporate training is very difficult unless you somehow produce a mass market product. The problem is that each project must be customized for the particular corporation. The software can be used again, but the content – or most of it – must change. Training departments of large corporations might want to add multimedia to existing training materials. In-store training kiosks can provide an on-line employee handbook. You can use multimedia for just-in-time training. By "just-in-time" we mean the ability for workers to get the information they need when *they* need it. Suppose your client needs a way to store technical drawings and schematics for after-sales repair work of a product. Conceptually, this is easy to do. You simply scan the necessary documents into your computer and apply a few animations to show, for instance, the assembly procedure. Now, repairs are faster and more accurate because the people in the trenches have better repair manuals at their disposal. Many companies, including Ben & Jerry's Homemade, Inc., Levi's Strauss, Northern Telecom, and Nike, all use multimedia-based training for in-house or customer uses.

Key Examples of Multimedia That Sell
INTERACTIVE EDUCATION

Computer and video games have been popular with children for a long time. Children and young adults compromise the market most accustomed to using multimedia. Children are the most likely demographic group to accept a multimedia work, to use the latest in technology, and to enjoy it.

Educators have come to realize that children will learn more if educational information is presented in a way that the student considers to be fun. By some estimates, pure educational titles make up about 25 percent of the current CD-ROM titles being sold. According to *Technological Horizons in Education (T.H.E.) Journal*, almost US$869 million will be invested by educational institutions in 1994 on multimedia equipment. This number represents an increase of 30 percent over the previous year and includes various products (such as speakers, CD-ROM drives, video cameras, sound cards, and videodisc players).

T.H.E. Journal tracks trends in the North American educational institutions, such as K—12 schools, colleges and universities, and industry and government training centers. *T.H.E. Journal's* research indicates that computer-centered multimedia learning technologies are now favored by educators. This is also a great area for hybrid works. "Infotainment" and "edutainment" are categories of educational hybrid works, and they are highly successful. If you want to enter the world of interactive education, infotainment and edutainment titles may be effective ways of getting your message across.

Always remember your audience. Do not try to remember what interested you when you were a child since you are no longer the audience. Ask today's children what interests and excites them and really listen to what they have to say. Find out what types of illustrations or characters they respond to, and create your own. Also listen to the group that will most likely be making the purchasing decision. Educators and parents will be influenced by what their children want, but these adults will not buy your product if your educational message does not come across effectively, or if your product contains excessive violence, sex, or discriminatory behavior. Cast your characters from a variety of minority and ethnic groups. These are very popular among educators who are continually being pressured to be politically correct.

The interactive element is very important. People learn more by doing than by seeing or hearing. The more your customer can be involved in making decisions about what to learn, how to learn, and how to use the information provided, the more he or she is likely to own that information. Children are sophisticated about interactive products, so put in plenty of action and do not allow more than 15 or 20 seconds go by without requiring them to choose what to do next.

Games

Games are a huge market. They are available in cartridge format as videogames such as Sega and Nintendo, on CD-ROM discs, or through on-line services such as America Online and CompuServe. There is a constantly expanding demand for multimedia games. Players tend to get bored with one game and want to move on to the next. This helps increase sales generally, but it takes a lot of time, money, and luck to create truly interesting games. Most of today's games are derived from math games or *Dungeons & Dragons* and other related interactive and problem-solving games. There is a science fiction and fantasy element related to many adventure games, and a mathematical flavor behind others.

To gain market share and spread the cost of creating, producing, and distributing, many small developers work with **affiliate label programs** to publish their first or second CD-ROM game disc. As we will discuss later in the book, marketing folks place affiliate label programs somewhere between self-publishing and completely turning your title over to a publisher along with all control over sales and marketing. Sony Electronic Publishing, Compton's New Media, Brøderbund, Discis, and Electronic Arts are a few of the affiliate label publishers in the market today.

AFFILIATE LABEL PROGRAMS
Programs that publish and distribute your CD-ROM title for you in return for a percentage margin of the sales price. Some affiliate label programs merely distribute your self-published title.

Certain affiliate label publishers will require a developer to sign an exclusivity agreement for a particular number of years or titles. This may provide you with a jump start to your career or it may severely limit your opportunities. Get as much information as you can, along with competent legal advice, before signing one of these agreements.

Music

What do Herbie Hancock, Peter Gabriel, David Bowie, and many, many others have in common? They all use multimedia as an extension and integral part of their musical career. Peter Gabriel, for instance, was one of the first musicians to incorporate the effects from his creative concert presentations into a CD-ROM called *XPLORA 1: Peter Gabriel's Secret World*. Now *you* want to make or invest into an interactive music CD-ROM. What do you need to know? Well, first of all, you need to know music. This sounds obvious but you would be surprised by the number of people who try to create things that they don't really understand.

XPLORA 1: PETER GABRIEL'S SECRET WORLD is an interactive tour of his works, life, and mind. You decide whether you want to try mixing a single from your computer keyboard, learning the history or sound of exotic African instruments, or simply let Gabriel guide you along his own path.

A music CD-ROM must have a clearly defined focus. This means that you must know who your target market is before you start creating the work. Music is highly personalized. You cannot necessarily define a particular musical taste by sex, class, or other demographic factors. You have to use the inherent qualities of the music itself to determine your market. Marketing experts at the major music companies have done extensive research to match their advertising and content to their target market. If you cannot afford to do your own research, you may wish to use the advertising focus defining the artist. Combine this with your own expertise (and that of your marketing people) to determine how multimedia technology can better present the music. Another successful joining of music and multimedia can be found at music stores. Kiosks, such as US-based *.i. station*, allow you to dial up your choice of music so that you can hear it before you buy. The kiosk includes portions from videos, as well as special animation and other graphics. The *.i. station* is an informational kiosk since the user receives information about a product but not the product itself. In fact, the function of this kiosk is marketing. It is implemented to increase sales.

Electronic Newsletters and Magazines

Increasingly, information providers are creating electronic newsletters and magazines. Typically, these take the form of CD-ROMs delivered regularly to your door. They can also be delivered by way of electronic information providers such as **CompuServe or America Online**. Not only are costs of production lower with the interactive versions of magazines, but media-rich information makes a greater impact. Stories can be brought to life using multimedia design principles.

COMPUSERVE AND AMERICA ONLINE
Privately run interactive bulletin board information systems connecting millions of individual computer users to the Internet.

Clearly there are problems with this distribution channel. Despite the fact that CD-ROM drive sales are large (Apple Computer, for instance, will have sold close to 3 million CD-ROM drives by year end 1994), not everyone has a CD-ROM drive or access to the Internet. On the other hand, just about everyone can read a traditional magazine. In addition, people are used to the feel of paper between their fingers. Besides, you can pull out a magazine anywhere. No one would take his or her electronic magazine – and the necessary computer hardware – into the bathtub. Still, you can make money as long as you target a receptive market. Computer professionals, engineers, on-line subscribers, and many teachers who are used to receiving information in electronic form are prime candidates for these newsletters and magazines. Market to those who are already sold on the technology. Let others blaze the trail for you.

Electronic Books

Pioneered by the Voyager Company and Discis Educational Research, electronic books are gaining popularity. These books are simply an extension of existing book content with multimedia features added to make them more fun. These books can be a great introduction to multimedia for children and parents alike. This is why children's books and readalongs have been the first wave of books to be transformed into digital form. However, adult titles can be extremely effective. Rick Smolan did a great job with *From Alice to Ocean*. This beautiful coffee-table book successfully blended the best aspects of producing books using electronic and conventional methods.

To be successful, ensure that your audience can use your book interactively and easily, but still sees your product for what it is – a book. Many developers make the mistake of using as many multimedia tricks as possible simply because they are there. Smart developers use multimedia to make the book more enjoyable to their readers. Electronic books are attractive because they combine the positive elements of paper books – interesting content – with the special elements that multimedia can offer. However, you cannot simply scan a traditional book into a computer, throw in a few illustrations, and call it an electronic book. No one will want to scroll through several pages of text so you must cut up your book into bite-size pieces and add video, audio, and interaction.

You also have to be careful when deciding what to transform into an electronic book. Children's books are ideal because they traditionally contain comparatively few words, short sentences, and straightforward ideas. You need to choose a subject and story that can benefit from multimedia through the addition of sound effects, interesting vocal tracks, music, video effects, the nesting of subjects into the story-line, or other tricks of the trade. You also have to choose a subject that won't get lost in the effects.

PRODUCTIVITY AND AUTHORING TOOLS

We're not going to tell you what tools you must use to create your multimedia work. That is the subject of other books. We do want to mention that there is money to be made by making tools for other developers. In fact, according to research sponsored by the Apple Multimedia Program, up to 33 percent of its developers are actively engaged in making multimedia-related tools. This means your tools must be very good to compete against the established competition. The real opportunity is not to improve on a tool offered by a major player, but to create a niche product that you discover missing from available tools. Don't forget that your tool must be completely compatible with the rest of the industry.

Consult Chapter 15 for books on the subject.

Chapter 3

Business Planning

This chapter concerns itself with the nuts and bolts of business planning. A business plan should contain the who, what, where, when, how, and how much of your business. Include a corporate vision in your business plan only in terms of how it relates to money-making. You have to know how to assess all sides of your company to present it in its best light without being misleading. We present a good way to structure your business plan, along with the most important elements to include and how to write about them. We also explain how to fill in the gaps in your skill set by establishing contacts in the community.

A sample business plan is included in Chapter 14.

Although this advice is tried and true, it won't make you an accountant or a finance MBA overnight. There's a reason why these folks go to school for years. Even after you read and study the material in this chapter, it may be useful for you to enroll in a short course at your local college or university. These courses are usually inexpensive and are sometimes taught at night or on weekends. Recognize that you must always customize any information you use in your statements and plans to the specific facts and needs of your company.

In Chapter 6, we present specific examples of multimedia financial statements.

General Overview of the Business Plan

You wouldn't start programming without some sort of plan. The same is true about your business. In fact, it is probably more important to have a sound business plan and proper accounting than it is to have a clear vision of your final product. The proper financing and accounting documents you need are explained in Chapter 6 and must be included in your formal business plan. You will need to demonstrate a clear understanding of your market and how you are going to sell your product or service to your market. Be direct. There is no length requirement. Just make sure that the important elements we describe in this chapter are covered.

Why You Need a Business Plan

Creating a business plan is an important process for the entrepreneur. It should contain a thorough analysis of your business including its place in the market, its competition, its financial status, its production and distribution mechanisms, its key employees, and its general strengths and weaknesses. It should also contain your vision for the future and a step-by-step description of how you are going to achieve your goals. By analyzing these factors and relating them to each other you will be able to determine a logical road to travel to make money. Be prepared for the worst. The business plan should tell you the cold, hard facts. The most logical step might be to abandon a particular venture that is unlikely to be profitable. In the end, a business plan helps to prepare you for whatever you may encounter in your venture.

But that's not all a business plan does.

Business plans are absolutely necessary to get external financing. Investors need to see where their money is going before they agree to invest or loan it. They need to know that your business venture is well thought out and likely to be profitable. Investors get virtually all their information about your business from your business plan. Don't expect to sell them on your product with a demo or a quick trip to the studio. They want documentation in a format they are used to. Make a clear, detailed, and complete plan or don't expect to get any money. Multimedia industry venture capitalists should demand detailed information in the proper format prior to investing.

A business plan is not just a ruse to get financing. It is a living tool for you to use as your business develops. Monitor the plan periodically to find out if you have exceeded expectations or failed to achieve goals. Analyze your results to find out why your business is succeeding or failing. Modify your business and your plan as necessary. Downsize or reorganize unprofitable ventures. Use the business plan as an honest mirror on your company. Your friends won't tell you but your business plan will.

Performance and Viability
Past Performance

Investors will be interested in your past performance as much – if not more – than your present status and future projections. If you are just starting out in a particular business, describe in detail your previous accomplishments in other ventures or companies. Do the same for your partners and others integral to your company. If you have no previous accomplishments, do not try to hide this fact. You can, however, concentrate on your education and the past successes of similar products or ventures.

Present Performance

Performance numbers are very important to investors. They should be divided into market performance, operating performance, and overall performance, because these show three distinct but important sides of the company. *Market performance* simply shows how well you are selling. Compare the returns from general operation with those that can be attributed to specific marketing events and promotions. That way you can assess your marketing strategies and results, and determine if they need to be modified.

Operating performance evaluates the performance of the company in terms of keeping costs of production down and keeping administrative costs low. General organization and corporate reorganization are all reflective of the market. Small companies are best suited to respond to changing market conditions because they have fewer layers of administrative bureaucracy to gum up the works. *Overall performance* combines the two assessments to evaluate how well the company is performing as a whole. If one side is doing far better than another, you will know where to concentrate your energies for reorganization.

Present Capabilities

Many multimedia companies try to be major players before their time. You probably cannot finance several projects right from the beginning. It takes time to market and sell your product, so don't expect your sales to grow instantaneously. Besides, your sales cannot grow at all unless you have the money to finance those sales. There are hard costs involved in making a multimedia product, and these costs have to be paid in advance before you can distribute and before any revenue is seen.

Consider the business cycle involved in making a kiosk, for example. First you have to find a customer with a kiosk requirement. Depending on your sales skills, economic conditions, your local market, and many other factors, this search can take a week or a few months. You then have to prepare a detailed analysis of your client's needs. Again, this could take days or weeks – it all depends on the complexity of the project. Once contracts are signed, you can start the development process. Next come the weeks of development time, storyboarding, and client status meetings to ensure everything is going as expected. During this time you have to support your staff, pay your rent and other overhead expenses.

Oh, you also have to eat during this whole experience. Long nights of programming and lots of late-night pizza do not make an attractive picture for your clients to see. Factor into your project costs a few days off just to relax and catch up with your personal life. Don't forget, you also have to finance the physical creation of the kiosk itself. All of these out-of-pocket expenses will likely create a financial strain on you. We recommend **milestone invoicing** to cushion the blow but, even so, you are looking at quite some time before you can see any of your money.

MILESTONE INVOICING
Cash management technique that divides large projects into small deliverables, each with an accompanying invoice.

Finally, if you are dealing with a very large corporation you might have to wait until the project is complete before you can invoice. And actual payment goes out after its 30-, 45-, or 60-day pay cycle. Unless you personally know the CEO, there is no way you can speed up this process – and asking for an exception to corporate policy can make you look naive and unprofessional. If you are dealing with a small company, you have to worry about the possibility of never getting paid if the company goes out of business. In all, it is likely that you will have to wait six months or more after the start of your project before you can collect any money at all. Potential investors have to see from your business plan that you can withstand this six-month waiting period. Financial plans are designed to prove this to potential investors and to keep you on track.

FUTURE VIABILITY

Every business plan specifies the amount and timing of cash requirements for the company. Few growing companies can survive by financing the growth through sales of the company. Multimedia business plans are different from traditional ones because cash requirements may tend to be higher than other companies of the same size. This is due, in part, to the technology necessary to perform certain multimedia-related tasks. Even though desktop video production technology is greatly reducing the costs of producing broadcast quality video work, for example, you still require expensive studio time to do your final edits and assembly. This is after you spend a fair bit of money acquiring the cameras, video equipment, sound equipment, computers and, of course, software.

Before you start your project, you need to determine how much cash you need. That cash must support all operating, development, marketing, and distribution costs. Time lines are useful in business plans and can be integrated to indicate cash infusion milestones or other important goals and objectives. By "time line" we simply mean a graphical line representing project time. This time line is usually divided into equal periods with annotations indicating actions and cash requirements. Some business plans use a vertical line to represent the passage of time within a project and then use text to indicate cash requirements by month or quarter.

Business Planning

We couldn't talk about business planning and cash requirements unless we talk about project management software packages. The larger multimedia projects usually indicate cash requirements as part of the overall business project plan. This is usually outlined by a specific budgeting section of the project management software package. These software packages are primarily designed to represent in picture format the project status. They also let you keep tabs on your project on a day-to-day basis. Project management software also tells your investors that you clearly understand the market and the business angles of multimedia by treating the project like a real business.

Another reason why we strongly endorse the use of project management software in multimedia is accurate **resource costing**. By using different mixes of resources (a more junior designer, for example, in place of your senior person), you may be able cut down some costs for your project. Of course, you can do all this with a calculator. Our experience tells us, however, that unless you use a computer and some easy-to-use project management software, resource costing won't get done.

RESOURCE COSTING
Resource costing tells you the actual cost of a particular part of your project by incorporating all the necessary resources (such as people, computers, time, bank interest) for that portion of the project.

Structure of the Business Plan

Start out with a concise and punchy executive summary. Try to leave out the fluffy adjectives since investors immediately ignore them anyway. The plan should include a brief description of the business, its market, and your vision for the future. Continue with an in-depth discussion of your intended market. The intended or target market should be described in terms of customer needs, wants, and general demographic profile. As well, you should outline how the company can satisfy those needs and wants in a timely, yet profitable, manner. If a demand for your product is not identifiable, a creative marketer will create the demand. Also included in this section should be an analysis of the competition and why you think prospective customers will buy from you and not from your more established competitors. Be brutal. It is far better to overestimate your competition in the marketplace than the reverse. Ask a trusted friend or other informed individual if you are sizing up the situation accurately.

Outline the management team and assets involved in your business. Describe your own qualifications and talents, as well as those of your partners and any others who are integral to your company. Relate these to what is needed to create a successful multimedia business. Also outline the major assets of the company and how they will be used to create a profitable venture. Your intangible assets may be your most important features. These are your contacts in the computer industry, your patents, trademarks and copyrights, your employment contract with a fantastically talented designer, or your exclusive right to license a software package for dentist offices, for example. It is hard to quantify these intangible assets, but try anyway so that you can present a more favorable description of your business. Formal business plans typically list education experience and degrees along with relevant employment details of everyone in the management team. In short, any factual information that will persuade a potential investor to give you money should be included.

Your plan should also contain financial projections and your own financial statements. But don't let the statements speak for themselves. Almost as important as the actual statements are the supporting documents explaining their meanings and the assumptions that you have used in creating them. Tell your readers where you get your facts. Mention independent studies if you have used them. The key is to be as straightforward and accurate as possible. People who read business plans have read it all before and can see a con job a mile away. Marketing and sales hype is only effective if it is backed up by independent facts. Ideally, you want to make your company and product appear more legitimate by using logical conclusions from indisputable sources.

STATEMENT OF PURPOSE

Figure out what business you're in – and stick with it. You might be surprised how many multimedia developers don't bother formalizing their company's purpose. Not only is a formal statement of purpose required in your business plan, it also keeps you on the straight and narrow. What do we mean by this? Multimedia, as a subsector within the computer, communications, and entertainment industries, represents a wide area of expertise.

If your company is relatively large, you can afford to diversify your business. Otherwise, specialize in one or a small number of technologies and platforms. To paraphrase an old expression, "You can't (or shouldn't attempt to) be all things to all people." By clearly outlining what you are and what your company does, you tell your customers what business you're in. You also tell them – and yourself – what business you're *not* in. Investors look for leaders and entrepreneurs who understand their strengths *and* their weaknesses. Your business plan should reflect this understanding.

BUSINESS ENVIRONMENT

Whether it is two pages or 200 pages (and somewhere in between is probably ideal), every business plan must describe the business environment in which the company operates. By this, we mean, you should know what challenges and opportunities your particular company faces in doing business. Outline the competitive companies and products in the industry. Describe any underground market that may cut into your market. Note your proximity to major centers of population, and outline how this affects your business. Describe whether or not your competition faces these same hurdles and *how* they face them. Describe your affiliation or sponsorship by a major company. Even in a rapid growth industry like multimedia there are business, regulatory, and other restrictions you must outline. Further, you must have a clear idea of how you plan to overcome these concerns so your business can operate profitably. The challenge in your particular case may be overcoming low market awareness of your product. The benefit may be that there is no competition for your market.

OWNERSHIP STRUCTURE

The business plan should also outline the ownership structure for your company. Investors and clients are heavily influenced by people they know. People do business with *people* and having a well-known or influential person in your company can only help you. Ownership structure also indicates to potential investors who are calling the shots and how much power they wield. Venture capitalists purchase a chunk of your company in exchange for some cash. Although it is very unlikely your venture capital people would purchase more than 50 percent of your company (after all, they are in the business of managing capital and making money – not running a multimedia company), they need to know who owns and is involved in your company before they commit to buying into it. As well, a business plan must have an **exit strategy** at your initial public offering stage to be taken seriously by a VC company.

EXIT STRATEGY
The process by which investors can remove their money from a company.

MANAGEMENT TEAM

Make sure that you have all the skills sets covered. In Chapter 1, we outlined some of the people involved in the Multimedia Food Chain. By organizing your business and creating a plan you can see which skills are covered and which are not. Your experience and education factor greatly in this section because one of the greatest predictors of the future is past performance. If you've been a manager, director, or producer in other multimedia firms, mention it here. Some people think they should include their résumé or CV in the business plan. This is not exactly true. In a résumé you generally list your skills and accomplishments to appeal to a wide variety of potential employers. In the management team description of the business plan you describe how your specific skills can be used to develop, manage, and expand the business.

Due to their traditional training, bankers and other investors may be very impressed by your five years at IBM, for example. Venture capitalists, on the other hand, are less impressed with the "big" firms and more interested if you've had direct (and profitable) experience doing your job at other multimedia companies.

PROJECT PLAN

As we mentioned before, each individual project requires its own plan. We strongly recommend a project management software package to manage your costing, staffing, and technical requirements. It doesn't really matter who you are and how big your operation is. You should always know where you stand financially. A project manager, an in-house developer, and your client need to know what parts of the project have been accomplished and what parts remain to be done. From an investment standpoint, firms who manage their projects closely and carefully make money consistently.

Marketing Plan

Marketing plans are logical outflows from business plans. Marketing plans specialize in outlining, discussing, and forecasting how the sales and marketing activities will most likely unfold. In the multimedia world, developing your product or service is typically front-end loaded. A large outlay of cash goes into the initial stage, which is hopefully followed by a large revenue stream.

Take, for example, a CD-ROM project. Before you start storyboarding the final product or writing the script, a marketing plan is in order. Just as business plans keep your business on track, marketing plans ensure products and services are released on time, on budget, and with enough marketing support to make a difference. If your business plan calls for the production of a CD-ROM, your investors will want to know why you chose a particular title or content. Who is likely to buy your finished disc and how do you intend on reaching these people? What kind of distribution model do you intend on using – one-tier, two-tier, three-tier? Why? How are you going to advertise and promote your disc? Will your customers want to buy your product 24 hours a day or just from 9 to 5, Monday to Friday? The marketing plan seeks to explain and answer these (and many other) questions in a compelling manner. Investors look for evidence that a company knows who its customers are and what motivates these customers to make a purchase decision.

If you're an in-house developer, your situation might be different. Your marketing plan might include how to implement and deploy your multi-media project throughout your company. Don't think that just because your audience is internal you don't have to sell yourself and your project. You have to be both an expert salesperson and a top manager to sell your project amid the political maneuvering and inter-departmental fighting that can take place in a large corporation.

Research and Development Plan

In a typical business plan there is always a section for research and development (R&D). This part of the business plan outlines any efforts your company is formally undertaking for the development and eventual sale of a new finished good, process, or service. If your company plans to release a new multimedia programming tool or video board, this is where you describe the development efforts and processes in hardware, firmware, and software. Describe your testing procedures, quality control, and methods of assuring accuracy. R&D expenses can eat up investment capital very quickly so it is important to let your financial backers – and yourself – know where the investment in R&D is going. There are several ways of forecasting R&D budget dollars, most of which match expenses with expected returns. Our recommendation is to create your R&D budget from your project management software output. By closely linking the two you will be able to track all important aspects of your project.

Most projects will take longer than expected. Never write an R&D plan on a critical path and always be prepared to scrap new development if your results show it to be unprofitable or counter-productive. However, don't be too quick to judge. Allow time for the cycle of development and feedback to run its course. R&D requires time, and time requires money. R&D money is an investment in your company's future profitability.

Staff and Locational Plan

The most important part of any multimedia project is the people. Finding the right ones is cause for celebration; the wrong ones will cause you grief. This is why just about all formal business plans outline the expected staffing needs for the company's immediate projects. Typically, investors look for strategic thinking in this section. If you envision going after some government markets, for example, it is advisable to hire someone who has experience working for or with the government.

A locational plan is helpful if your company's success depends on being at a certain place at a certain time. Let's imagine for a moment your company designs and produces kiosk-based multimedia projects. You have clients who require guaranteed service at any location throughout the country. Without outlining a locational plan, in this case, for servicing and updating your kiosks, your business plan is incomplete and risks getting rejected by potential investors. A locational plan is usually connected with your marketing plan since the sales and distribution strategy you propose in your marketing plan will dictate the type of locational plan you use.

FINANCIAL PLAN

We've saved the best part of the business plan for the end. The financial plan quantifies the forecasts from the previous sections of the business plan. There's no "best way" to present your information physically, but we want to tell you about some of the most effective ways.

For a quick reference, look at the examples of financial statements we present in Chapter 6. Your financial plan will not look exactly like this as you must customize it to your own business needs. The important thing to understand is the feel of a financial plan. Numbers won't tell the whole story, but they are extremely important to support any claims that you have made. That means you must emphasize the most important numbers and calculations. You must present a break-even analysis that shows the minimum amount of revenue you will need to earn in a variety of scenarios if you are to make enough money to cover costs. These scenarios can present a range of different prices for the product or service, a range of different purchasing results, and other options. You must include best and worst case scenarios to project if your business is likely to be profitable. These will also show how profitable the business might be, and how much investors really risk. Make sure your projections are based on well-researched facts and not on your hopes and dreams. Any good investor will be able to see through a faulty financial plan.

Which brings us to the investor side. If you are considering investing in a multimedia project or company, or joining such a company, review the financial plan carefully. This is not the time for you to dream either. Find out where assumptions have been made and check the facts behind these assumptions. Most importantly, find out the track record of the management team. Contact people with whom they have worked previously. Don't just accept claims of higher education or business titles. Anyone can have a fancy business card.

How Multimedia Business Plans Differ from Traditional Business Plans

Traditional businesses produce a simple product or a known service. Their originality generally comes in their marketing or, in rare cases, in the simple product itself. Multimedia products are generally distinctive. Presentation is unique because the products are individually programmed. Content should be unique as it is generally obtained from an independent source.

Multimedia services and products are also unique because they are intangible. Most people are still used to the concept that bigger is better. Getting your prospects to wrap their brains around the fact that a single two-ounce disc is better than 26 heavy books, for example, can be a real challenge. Just because your product is the greatest thing since video tape does not mean that the public will rush out to buy it. You must always factor into your plan the reluctance of the general public to adopt something new. Remember who won the war between Beta and VHS.

Having said that, CD-ROM title sales are a multimillion-dollar business, kiosks are springing up all over, and more and more people are using multimedia in all facets of their businesses. The Digital Information Group estimated that 1993 CD-ROM title sales reached nearly US$6 billion worldwide. The most successful sellers of these products and services are those who incorporate something highly recognizable into their products. Other games might be more interesting than those by Sega but everyone wants to play with *Sonic the Hedgehog* because everyone else does. The games market that started with *Pong* grew to a corporate best-seller with Atari, went on to Nintendo and is now dominated by Sega. Sega and Nintendo combined have an installed base of over sixteen million game players. Who knows who will be successful next year! The monolithic companies have the marketing budget to make a *Super Mario Brothers* movie and to ensure that you recognize a Sega ad. You probably don't have anything approaching their budget, so try to work with someone who holds the rights to a recognizable piece of media or to obtain the rights yourself.

How to Find People to Fill in the Gaps in Your Skill Set

Find out the abilities of the people already around you. Copy writers, designers, and programmers could have gained their experience in related industries. However, you want your project manager, lawyer, and marketing expert to have experience in the multimedia world.

To find people to work on your project or business, you have to go where they gather. Major multimedia trade shows and conferences bring together most of the industry experts and beginners. Approach those writing for trade magazines and newspapers. Even if they are not available to join your team, they will probably be able to steer you in the right direction. Finally, colleges and universities are a great training ground for up-and-coming animators, graphic designers, and the like. You may be able to convince a talented designer to apprentice with your company to gain experience or just to get an opportunity to work in the industry.

For a list of these trade shows, consult Chapter 15.

Chapter 4

Marketing 101

"This product sells itself!"
"If you build it, they will come."
"Advertising is all hype. It's the product that counts."

Back on this planet, marketing is an integral part of any project, and a necessity to succeeding in business.

What Marketing Means

Marketing means a lot of things. It means research. It means thoroughly understanding who is out there to buy your product or service, and positioning your product or service to catch their attention. It means knowing what your audience likes and dislikes. Marketing also means working with distributors. It means product design and packaging. Marketing means deciding how much to charge, and determining the level of quality and sophistication your buyers demand. Marketing means creating a company image for the press and the general public. Marketing means taking your company from production to sales. Marketing puts you on a course that can determine where the sales force should focus their efforts. Marketing is the compass you use to find money.

Corporations use formal presentation documents when they are introducing a new product or project. Marketing requirements documents (MRDs) outline the elements involved in the marketing of a product from demand to distribution. Program requirements documents (PRDs) concentrate on projects or services. These documents include extremely detailed information from every department. Each key player or department includes a section detailing how their input will contribute to the success of the product or project. Research reports should be analyzed and summarized for the document. There should be descriptions and drawings of the product, its packaging, and precisely how they will fit together. Delivery schedules, support and services offered, and the key events to be used to leverage marketing (such as trade shows) should be included.

Many multimedia products involve foreign or outside involvement, so one section should take the reader on a tour of the different locations from which the product eventually comes together. A very important section comprises charts, graphs, and related analysis. Price will be graphed against performance for the product, other products in the same general line, and competing products. From this key information, decision-makers can determine whether the introduction of the product or project is successful or whether they need to consider a new marketing direction.

Using the Business Plan

Marketing should be a full section in your business plan. You need to budget for marketing activities consistently throughout your project. Most multimedia products require a long investment of time. Programming and designing are painstaking tasks that require many hours at your keyboard. However you cannot forget about all other elements of the business while concentrating on the production.

You need to develop business relations with potential clients, customers, and distributors. You need to send out periodic press releases. You need to keep up appearances at industry functions such as trade shows and conferences. Most importantly, you have to gather feedback about your product to help you determine how to modify it as you go along. Finding out after your project is complete that you should have used a different interface, for example, can be a disaster. It is much simpler (and less expensive) to correct any problems early on in the project.

As well, you need to relate your methods of marketing to your ultimate corporate goals. If you want to sell interactive safety presentations for teenagers, your marketing should include music, language, and characters to which modern teens will respond. A multimedia title for accountants may have some dry humor, but should be relatively serious and project-oriented. A scantily clad beach bunny will not sell multimedia products to preschoolers.

Advertising

For that matter, you shouldn't be using anything scantily clad to sell your product or service. You are far too likely to offend large portions of your market with obviously discriminatory advertising. Even though there is a market for multimedia products involving sexual or violent situations, adding sex or violence to your product's advertising will not guarantee sales or success. In fact, gratuitously throwing either of these into your advertising will likely turn off today's customers. Using such questionable and misleading advertising gimmicks will only cause your customers to be disappointed in the product they buy. You will get negative reviews and you will find it difficult to sell your next product.

Advertising is big business, but you certainly don't need a huge budget and a major ad firm to advertise your product successfully. Some of the lowest-budget commercials with the cheesiest production values have become obscenely profitable in the form of infomercials. You don't need to go as far as making a 30-minute or even a 30-second commercial. Your product may have a focused customer base that will respond well to a direct mail campaign. Maybe you can reach your customers through a publicity stunt at a trade show, a medieval fair, or a football game. The important thing to remember is to know and understand your market. Mass marketing is only effective for products that are being mass distributed. Virtually everyone drinks Coca-Cola and the Coca-Cola Company spends lavishly to market its product to everyone. You, on the other hand, have a more specific target market in mind. Concentrate your marketing focus.

For example, you are producing a CD-ROM about birds. Call up bird-watching magazines, tell them about your product, and try to get them to write an article about it. At the very least, they will probably mention your CD-ROM in their "What's New" section. Call up bird-watching clubs – local, national, and international – to get an opportunity to show your product to them, and to be included in their newsletters. Send free copies of your CD-ROM to the presidents of the clubs, the publishers of the magazines, and other important people in the bird-watching community. Just as your product and audience are focused, your advertising and marketing must be focused as well.

How Marketing Equals Leverage

Some people say that marketing is sales when your sales department can't be there. Marketing creates the pull to make suspects into prospects, whereas sales convert prospects into customers, as we will discuss in the next chapter. Leverage is the process by which you can accomplish a lot with a small effort. In marketing terms, we use leverage to mean the ability to target, reach, and sell to customers with minimal effort and resources.

What can you do with a small budget? If you have a baseball CD-ROM, sponsor a local team, contact the closest professional club and organize a **cross-promotional event.** You can also send out free copies to the sports editors, writers, or anchors in your area. If you have a fashion kiosk at the local shopping mall, call up the news and color editors of the major papers and magazines to tell them about your product. Send out press releases and demo discs. Get into the mall advertising circular. Set up a kiosk at fashion shows. There are hundreds of things you can do to make your company or product name recognizable. Don't rest until everyone who might buy your product knows how it can change his or her life.

> **CROSS-PROMOTIONAL EVENT**
> Marketing activities done by more than one company in tandem where both companies' products are complementary or related.

Don't forget about user groups, especially if your product is inexpensive. A user group is simply a collection of people who use the same product and get together periodically to discuss it. User groups like to feel that they are in the know. Exploit this by giving them inside information on how your product works.

The owners of recognizable trademarks like Microsoft Word or Lotus 1-2-3 have marketing leverage. People buy these products because they have heard of them, and because everyone else buys them. Disney Studios has marketing leverage as well, because its characters are instantly recognizable to the public. You can create your own marketing leverage by working with something recognizable. Approach companies or people with recognizable characters, locations, writings, or anything else that you can incorporate into your multimedia project. Many established companies are willing to license their property or participate in a joint venture for a percentage of the profits. In short, you will get the right to leverage their recognizable assets for a set price or a percentage. However, you can bankrupt yourself if you become obsessed with getting a particular piece. Make sure the price is worth the anticipated benefit.

Marketing Is a Big Picture Activity whereas Sales Is One-on-One

Creating the look and feel of your product is one component of marketing. Showing the finished package to a prospective customer is part of sales. In marketing, you have to anticipate the customer's reaction to both the product and to the marketing. Don't assume that you are your market. Buyers for your product may be widely diverse so don't pigeonhole your product into a particular niche unless that niche contains every possible customer.

Marketing is not concerned with how many sales were made today. Marketing is concerned with how many sales can be made in the long run. You achieve sales through successful marketing campaigns.

MARKETING STARTS BEFORE YOU DO ANYTHING ELSE

People come up to us at trade shows asking how they can market their product. Our first question is, "Where are you in your development cycle?" (Actually our first question is, "How much will you pay us if we tell you?") Far too many tell us that they have finished their product. They have no budget left and they mistakenly think that buyers should come to their doors begging to buy the product. Don't fool yourself. This will not happen.

Many fantastic products never get off the ground because their developers don't give a thought to marketing until the product is completed. You don't have to finalize your product before you figure out how to market it. A great deal of marketing work goes into determining the product design itself. The interface must be neither too complicated nor too simplistic for your market. How will you know what your customers will understand if you don't know who your customers are?

Several market research firms are listed in Chapter 15.

Children tend to respond well to certain types of animation, depending on their ages. The youth market is also very sophisticated in terms of responding to 3-D effects, realism, and digitally manipulated images. Terms that are used everyday in London may not be understood in Los Angeles. These are some of the many factors that go into determining both design and content. Localization and targeting are extremely important. This is why you must do your market research before spending everything you have on creating something you don't know how to sell.

MARKETING SETS YOUR GOALS

In the last chapter we explained how you set your overall goals in the business plan. Marketing plans take your overall goals and translate them into an action plan for success. In a way, we are talking about drilling down a layer. We go from a business plan to a marketing plan to making sales.

Marketing plans tend to focus on product introductions, implementations, distribution strategy, pricing, and other big picture activities. It's important to be able to set goals with your team. There are several different models upon which to base your marketing plan. Most of these models boil down to the same issues: objectives, strategies, and tactics.

What does this mean for a multimedia company? Say your company creates business presentations. A company objective may be to become more efficient (and profitable) in producing these business presentations. Be careful, however, not to keep spinning your wheels. If you receive a good profit for each business presentation but only sell a few of them, a better objective might be to increase the number of business presentations your company sells.

Setting goals using models may seem silly, but it works. The figure below shows a simple objectives, strategies, and tactics (OST) chart outlining a hypothetical business presentations company.

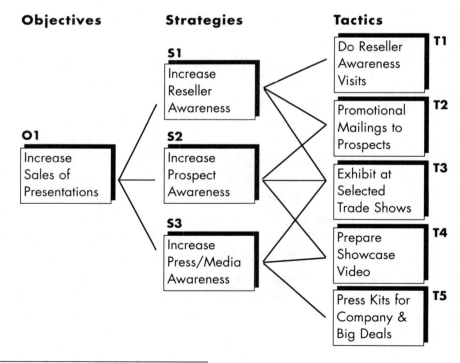

The purpose of any business is to make money, but there are many different ways to make money. The more people in your company and the more complex your business, the more likely the goals will be forgotten. The OST chart helps to keep you focused and helps you understand how the activities you do during the day relate to one another and how these help the company survive and succeed.

Objectives

By objectives, we mean the specific objectives at the heart of the company. If a company's primary objective is to increase sales, then the company's efforts must be focused on that. The company cannot effectively focus on corporate expansion and increasing productivity at the same time unless the company is a conglomerate. Most companies can only focus on one or two objectives at a particular time. For this reason, it is important to choose your main objectives carefully to obtain the best results.

Obviously, the best objective for any particular company depends on the strengths and weaknesses of that company. Look at the corporate and administrative structure of your company. Is there a great deal of duplication? Is there excessive administration? Is there no administration? Do you get completely immersed in one project and neglect to continue prospecting for your next customer?

Consider our original example of a business presentations company. All your managers meet one Monday morning and start brainstorming – throwing every idea on the table about how to get more revenue into the company. After much discussion, it is agreed that the first objective of the company is to sell more business presentations. The managers must then shift their attention to *how* they can accomplish their goal.

Strategies

Objectives are what you want. Strategies are the plans to get what you want. Back at the meeting, your objective is to sell more presentations and a number of logical strategies are discussed. One manager notes a fair number of good leads come from certain computer resellers in the city. Another manager thinks that insufficient prospects know about you and what you do. Finally, your marketing expert says that the press is always on the lookout for good stories about local high-tech companies. Your strategies might be: to target market the resellers producing good leads, to direct market companies that could use your services, and to cultivate press relations.

As you can see, your strategies depend on your original objective(s) *and* on your company's resources. If you are a small shop, don't bother blowing your whole budget on a major trade show. Even if you *could* compete with the industry giants that have massive show budgets and buy huge tracts of booth space, you probably couldn't follow up on the hundreds of sales leads anyway. You have to be smart and choose your fights. If you've picked your strategies well, you should be able to design reasonable tactics to market your multimedia project successfully.

Tactics

Tactics are the precise details employed to get what you want. Let's say you decide your company has enough **marketing bandwidth** for five tactics to carry out your three strategies. First, to increase computer reseller awareness you plan to schedule some visits to local dealers in your territory. Most computer dealers hold weekly meetings to discuss existing accounts and sales plans, new or upcoming products, and administrative matters. Book yourself into these meetings, make the rounds and tell each reseller about your services. By doing so, you indirectly expand your sales force. It wouldn't hurt to offer them a finder's fee for each client they bring you. One word of warning, however. Always talk to the manager in charge first.

MARKETING BANDWIDTH
The overall capabilities of your company and its marketing budget.

Many managers resent so-called third party "**spiffs**" because they feel these spiffs interfere with the smooth operation of *their* business and the successful implementation of their company's objectives, strategies, and tactics. Ask beforehand and you'll be treated right.

> **SPIFFS**
> Special incentives used to induce salespeople to concentrate on your particular product.

Another tactic might be to do a mailer to a select, well-researched target market. Look at your existing customers and find others with the same qualities. Many mailing houses will sell or rent you one use of their categorized lists for pennies a name. These names are usually culled from various sources including industry memberships and trade show attendees. They represent a significant value if they are used wisely.

Product Marketing

Product marketing means structuring your marketing programs around a specific product or group of products instead of the company itself. Marketing focuses on the features and benefits of your product, often in comparison to that of your competition. Let's say your company sells blank recordable CD-ROM discs that are less expensive and less prone to failure than other discs in the market. (Remember to be very sure of your facts and your documentation before you make any claims.) Using a product marketing strategy, you design a campaign to reach your target market — in this case developers of CD-ROMs, in-house corporate developers and, perhaps, network managers needing to archive their data. In this campaign you compare your discs to the competition. The Pepsi Challenge is a classic product marketing campaign where Pepsi randomly asked people which glass of cola they preferred after drinking unmarked glasses of Coke and Pepsi. Those that selected Pepsi were then shown on television. A product marketing strategy is mostly used for simple products that have a clear, predictable use. For a more complicated product, your potential customers have to be told the benefits of using your product or service. This is where solutions marketing comes into the picture.

Solutions Marketing

When you have a complex product or solution that needs explaining, you typically use solutions marketing to get your message across. You determine what your customer needs or wants, and design your campaign around these factors. Let's say you manage a computer store. Market research tells you that customers need a desktop video authoring package. Using solutions marketing you could contact major vendors and tell them you intend to put together a bundle for desktop video editing. Ask them to put together a **bundle price** for their products in exchange for inclusion in the bundle and support. Collateral material like brochures and solution sheets could be subsidized by the vendors as well. Finally, the vendors might actually help you sell the bundle by sending their sales reps to your store or office, or allowing you a small space in their booth at a local trade show. In this example, the larger your company, the more likely you are to convince the vendors of the advantages of this plan.

BUNDLE PRICE

Often called the original equipment manufacturer (OEM) price, this low price is given to bulk purchasers of a product for inclusion in their bundle of related products.

An example of a bundle that worked was the Apple Professional Video Production Solution. This combines the products of six hardware manufacturers and software developers for an all-in-one video production package. The elements included were two AppleDesign Powered Speakers; Adobe Premiere, a video editing package; a 2-gigabyte array from Storage Dimensions for extremely fast hard drive storage and retrieval; digidesign Audiomedia II sound card hardware and software; VideoVision Studio by Radius, an advanced video editing and capture card; and VideoFusion's special effects software. All of these products were specially tested and chosen to work together. No computer system was included as it was anticipated that the market for a bundle of this nature would already have appropriate base hardware. The end result was a set of products combined in a single unit, providing everything a targeted market could want at a discounted price.

When you create a strategy using solutions marketing you try to make everybody win. You position yourself as a leader in the solutions marketplace and your vendors are seen as part of a complete and workable solution for their customers.

Press Relations

When you are thinking about marketing, realize that the press can be your greatest marketing tool if you apply a concentrated effort. The press (generally the people who deal with the printed word like newspapers and magazines) and media (people who make their living with the spoken word) are constantly looking for stories. They want to hear from you. If you are developing a new product, tell the review editors of the trade papers about it. If you are expanding your services, call the writers of your clients' corporate newsletters.

Chapter 12 covers press and media relations in more detail.

You should have a constant stream of *relevant* press releases going to a wide variety of people in the media. Create a database of technology magazines, newspapers, and newsletters. Streamline these, weeding out those that have too narrow a focus, unless that focus is on your product or market. Add to your database those publications that relate directly to your products or services. Bridal magazines may be more interested in your wedding planner software than magazines targeting computer engineers.

Write letters to the editor. Go to trade shows and meet people. Write articles *yourself* about general topics in your industry. There are many ways to get mentioned in the media. Don't be shy about taking advantage of them. Think! Get creative. Look at how others do it, and then do it better. Remember: people cannot buy your product if they do not know that it exists.

Chapter 5
Introduction To Sales

In the last chapter we talked about designing a marketing plan for your multimedia product or service. This is the chapter where you put your money where your mouth is. While marketing is a strategy, sales is a tactic. Without sales, the best product or service won't produce any revenue. Selling isn't that tricky, but it takes background work and a lot of patience.

The most effective salespeople are not slick hucksters who want to zoom in for the kill and bag the customer. Rather, the best salespeople are those who know their product, their market, and their customers thoroughly. Because of this background, they can effectively communicate their genuine belief in what they are selling. There are always reasons for buying your product or service. Successful salespeople concentrate on these reasons.

Selling Multimedia

Most multimedia developers believe the multimedia aspects of their project can sell the project itself. Unfortunately, this is not likely to be the case. Many people need to be sold; that is, they must be convinced that your product or service is essential to their business or life. They also have to be convinced that your product or service is better than that of your competitors. Depending on the individual, "better" might mean the project contains more functions or content, or is faster, cheaper, more compatible, or easier to use.

Selling multimedia is unlike selling anything else. Many people are unfamiliar with using multimedia technology. This lack of familiarity often intimidates potential customers. They might fear they will not be able to understand the technology or that it will break down. They might fear that it will not be compatible with their present system or that they do not have the physical tools to use it effectively. *You* have to know the technology from every angle to combat their objections. *You* have to be able to communicate highly technical concepts in simple language.

Selling multimedia is also just like selling anything else. You research your customer base to determine the needs, capabilities, and sophistication of your prospective customers. You should also find out how much your prospective customers can afford to spend on your product. You concentrate your efforts on those who can benefit from the product *and* can afford it. You meet with these prospects and explain why they should buy the product. You close the sale. If applicable, you provide after-sales support. Remember, multimedia is just an aspect of the project. What you are selling is the product or service itself. It just happens to contain multimedia to make it look good, to facilitate communication, or both.

Multimedia products and services are sold through a variety of different channels. Computer stores, bookstores, and specialty shops sell titles featuring multimedia content. These titles are also available through bundling. However, mail order, catalog, and telephone sales are one of the largest channels for multimedia titles on CD-ROM. Multimedia content is also sold electronically through various bulletin board systems and on-line services. On-line services might be the sales venue for your product if you are careful enough to protect your rights as you go along.

Bundling and other distribution options are covered in Chapter 7.

Selling Multimedia Services

Selling services, as opposed to products, can be hard work. This is because many people have become accustomed to seeing the product before they buy. It's hard to quantify a service, so it's hard to justify its price in any real terms. You have to prove the likely benefit of your service to your prospect. The way to justify the costs and overcome the objections, therefore, is to have testimonials and other examples showing the effects of your service. For instance, you can show off the effect and value of a multimedia presentation by showing a multimedia presentation about yourself and your services. Include testimonials from satisfied customers whom your prospects can call for references. Don't invent admiring customers or have your friends do the testimonials because prospects *do* check. You don't have to go overboard with your presentation. It can be a simple **HyperCard stack**, or even a video. It's true that you have to spen money to make money, but your don't have to spend all your money.

HYPERCARD STACK
A "stack" of electronic index cards forming a multimedia database.

Sales Levels

Realize that there are different levels in the sales process. For instance, at the industrial level, sales people generally deal with goods in their basic form. That is, goods that are mined, refined, or otherwise involved with the industrial process. In the computer industry, industrial companies are those that create programming tools or chips. Characteristically, this sales group spends long periods traveling within an established customer base – frequently for weeks on end, and often by air.

At the manufacturing level, we have the major hardware vendors like Apple. These businesses take the programming tools, plastic cases, disk drives, and other elements to create a finished good. Salespeople at this level also travel a great deal – typically by car. Generally they deal with distribution channels, but in some cases they may deal directly with the retailers.

Introduction to Sales

It's important to note that both industrial and manufacturing level salespeople typically deal with professional purchasing agents. Although these agents place the actual orders, savvy salespeople at this level are aware that the buying decision comes from departments such as engineering or administration. To be successful, therefore, these salespeople will determine who the decision-makers really are in the organization and include them in their sales efforts.

The third sales level is the distributor. Major computer hardware vendors and software developers typically sell through distributors. Distributors take large quantities of a product (a forklift full, or a skid) and repackage it into individual units for retailers. If you want to sell your CD-ROM title, for example, you may be able to leverage your sales efforts and maximize your revenue potential through a distribution company. Large distributors can include your product in a catalog seen by thousands of people. The down side of using a large distributor is that your product will likely be lost in the 30,000 other products being sold. Besides, the distributor will demand a large sales discount off the retail price – often 50 percent or more – to include your product in their catalog. Frequently, much of this discount is passed on to the next level of sales, leaving very little for the distributor. Smaller distributors may only have a handful of products, so yours will get more attention. The down side here is that small distributors cannot afford services such as a 24-hour telephone order line, and may not be able to capture a significant market share.

Chapter 15 contains a list of selected distributors.

The final level is retail sales, with which everyone is familiar. In the multimedia industry, retail salespeople sell CD-ROMs, multimedia software products, computer systems, and other consumer products. An initial small run of your product can be sold directly to retailers to test the market. If this is successful, you will have evidence for distributors and financiers to prove that your product is saleable. In general, if your product is being sold in a retail location, it is important to ensure that the salespeople are well informed about how your product works and why it is better than your competitor's. Demo samples, point of sale racking, and **collateral** are especially important at the retail sales level.

> **COLLATERAL**
> Glossy brochures, promotional material, and other sales aids designed to create more customer sales push and drive sales at the consumer level.

How to Find Prospects

Many developers sell direct to the customer and avoid both the retail and the distributor levels. This is because, for a typical CD-ROM disc, the dollar margin of the sale is low. That is, you have to sell a lot to make a lot because the product is relatively inexpensive. However, if you *are* using the distribution and retail sales levels, you probably don't have to worry as much about prospecting for customers, although you will naturally have to continue your marketing efforts. All you have to do, from the sales aspect, is to hook up with your **channel partners**, communicate your sales vision, supply them with sales collateral (such as brochures), and wait for the revenue to come in. Don't have false expectations. Even if you have done all you can to prepare a great product, there is no guarantee that the market will respond the way you want or plan.

> **CHANNEL PARTNERS**
> Industry term to describe computer resellers and others involved in the sales distribution process.

If you are selling a multimedia service, determine the characteristics of those who can best use your service. Research and find the customers that fit your description. If you specialize in creating kiosks, for example, you might be looking for a target company that provides the same or similar types of information to its customers on a regular basis. Another desirable characteristic might be that the company would benefit from increased hours of customer service, preferably without having to pay the labor and overhead usually associated with longer hours. Perhaps your prospect wishes to develop or keep a reputation for being a leader in technology. All these factors should be uncovered by your research. The most important fact to determine is whether your prospect can pay for the development and implementation of a kiosk.

Who fits these categories? Kiosks are already widely used in banks, tourist bureaus, and large retail outlets. Transit systems, music stores, museums, real estate companies, and many other businesses or government service agencies are starting to enter the multimedia world. Opportunities exist with these and many other parallel markets that may not have previously considered multimedia. The job of a salesperson is to introduce these prospects to multimedia kiosks and show them how technology can benefit them.

Preparation and Presentation

Get to know your product inside and out. You must have a sales plan and be prepared for all possible questions and objections. Multimedia products and services do not speak for themselves. It's a good idea to prepare a demonstration for prospects that shows how the product or service can benefit the purchaser. Use testimonials, comedy, action, and anything else that are likely to keep your prospect's interest.

If you decide to sell direct, you may wish to have an inside sales force of telemarketers to take orders or to make sales. Inbound telemarketers take the orders and start fulfillment. Outbound telemarketers typically work from a list and a script provided by the company. They make telephone calls to people without a sales history with the company or product. These are called cold calls. To make these calls, telemarketers require steely determination and the ability to deal with constant rejection. The best preparation is to convince yourself that you are doing your prospects a service by introducing them to something that can make their life simpler and more exciting, and make their business more profitable.

Do not stick rigidly to your sales plan or script, even if you are telemarketing. The personal touch is the factor that separates those that scrape by from those that make serious money. This is true in every type of sales, and multimedia is no exception. Your presentation should be slanted not only toward what you are trying to sell, but also to the individual characteristics of your customer. Successful salespeople ask existing customers what convinced them to make the purchasing decision. That way they can hone their sales pitch, accelerate the sales cycle, and make more money.

An objection is anything standing in the way of making a sale. Professional salespeople are adept at ferreting out these objections, and overcoming them. Once you establish that your prospect is ready, willing, and able to buy, the only thing standing in the way of making a sale is an objection. At this point the customer is "qualified." In the multimedia world, the main objections are: expense (sell them on the value), compatibility (sell them on the benefits), and complexity (show them how easy it is). If you can find no objection to closing the sale, and yet the prospect still refuses to make the purchase, he or she is probably not properly qualified.

Service After the Sale

Depending on your multimedia product, you have to design a support and service infrastructure to meet your customer's needs and expectations. Don't forget to factor the costs of after-sale service into your total production costs. Typically, if a CD-ROM is defective it is simply replaced by a working copy. Kiosks and business presentation software are another thing entirely. There is generally a warranty period of a year written into the contract during which time you must service the product if bugs are found. Service providers generally must live up to a level of quality based on the specific services they have agreed to perform. In both cases, you must make sure that your customer knows in advance exactly what he or she is getting and how to use what you provide.

If the product is not plug-and-play, you should have a training period in which you teach your customers how to use the product. Otherwise, they will be calling you every five minutes with yet another seemingly trivial question that wastes your time and theirs. Not only do these questions make your customers less satisfied with you, but they also interfere with your prospecting activities. A little time spent training your customers can make them completely satisfied with your product. A satisfied customer can be your best sales agent.

Getting Paid

Salespeople either get paid a wage or a commission, or a combination of both. You should structure your compensation for your sales staff in line with industry norms. You also have to determine your pay scale in relation to what you expect to make from the sale. If your staff is selling a CD-ROM for $19.95 and the net cost of the disc is $14.95, then you cannot give your sales staff a commission of 25 percent or there will be no revenue left over for you. Combine your collection activities with further prospecting. Introduce new services or opportunities with your bill. The sales cycle never stops – it just moves from one customer, product or service to the next.

Chapter 6
Introduction To Finance

Multimedia projects require lots of hard work and time before any revenue is produced. They also require hardware, software, general supplies, expert advice, as well as potentially costly content. Since all of these must be paid for in advance, the project must be financed in advance. That's where the art of finance comes in. One of the most important parts of finance is accounting. You have to know how to budget effectively, how to record your expenditures, and how to analyze your financial numbers. Keeping good accounting records allows you to understand your own financial position. This will show you not only your present status, but also how you got there, and what specific elements are keeping you down or keeping you afloat.

The Importance of Finance

To make money on any project, you must have a good idea of how much the project will cost. You must go through an extensive budget analysis of any particular project before you can give your client an estimate or determine for yourself if the project will be profitable. You have to know if you can afford to develop it on your own or if you need help. If you need a bank loan or other financing, you will need to show a complete set of detailed financial documents. Investors or lenders are not interested in you, per se. They want to know how much money they will make if they invest in your business.

If you're new to financial statements, you may find them intimidating. Many fledgling entrepreneurs want to leave their finances solely in the hands of professionals. Professionals should be consulted, but investors want to know that *you* — the person in charge — know how the money will be made. Besides, trusting *all* your financial concerns to others is never a good idea. At the very least, you should be able to understand, in a general way, your own financial statements. If you can't tell a balance sheet from a bed sheet this chapter will help you understand what bankers, investors, and other financial people mean when they say they want to see "your numbers."

Listed corporations are required to produce and file annual reports. Every corporation is required to prepare detailed financial documents for tax purposes. You will want to **incorporate** to limit your legal liability against debts and lawsuits. Incorporation won't help you if you act maliciously or fraudulently, but it acts as a first layer of insurance for accidents and business failure. Some multimedia developers don't incorporate to avoid the expense and increased paperwork. This is a mistake. The benefits and protection that incorporation offers far outweigh the drawbacks.

INCORPORATE
Formally filing registration papers with a federal, state, or provincial government to make your business into a corporation.

Incorporation is not prohibitively expensive or complicated. Filing fees are less than US$500, or a lawyer can take care of everything for about US$1000. In the United States and Canada, you will have to update your basic information every year by filing a simple standard government form and paying a small filing fee. As a corporation, you have to file corporate tax returns. As an unincorporated business, you have to file an incredibly complicated personal tax return. If you incorporate, corporate tax accounting can allow you to defer income tax for a longer period. However, strictly from a tax perspective, a company that is losing money in any particular year is better off unincorporated. That way, principals can deduct losses against any outside personal income. The benefits of incorporation are limitation of liability, potential tax deferral, and perception by customers that you own a more established business.

But even if you aren't incorporated, you should get into the habit of clearly documenting all financial expenditures and making realistic projections for the future. If you are working on your own, in partnership, or with friends, you might think that recording who spends what is a waste of time. After all, the project will soon produce so much money that everyone will have more than enough, right? Think again. Disagreements about money can tear apart the best friendships, families, and working arrangements. Write down from the beginning what each party is expected to contribute in terms of finances, equipment, and labor. Write down what share of the profits each party will get. Even if you don't have a formal shareholders' or partnership agreement, some form of documentation will save you from endless grief in the future.

Annual reports generally contain four financial statements: the income statement, the balance sheet, the statement of retained earnings, and the statement of changes in financial position. Any good accounting software package will generate these financial statements. Ask your accountant to suggest the best one for your particular situation. It should not only fit your type of business, but it should also be compatible with your accountant's own software. The particular method of entering your numbers will vary depending on the software you choose. We want to talk about how to read the financial statements and how to make judgments based on them. Our goal is to put you in a position so that you can actively improve your business through a thorough understanding of your financial position.

The Income Statement

Also known as the profit and loss statement or simply, the P&L, this document summarizes the revenues and expenses of your business over a certain time period. Net income, or profit, is the amount you get if you subtract your expenses from your revenues. If you have more expenses than revenues then you have a net loss, and a problem. You construct an income statement to figure out whether or not you are making any money.

Most people think that if you are taking in revenue you are making money. This is not necessarily true. Review the sample income statement on the next page. The book value of your company's assets diminishes through depreciation, insurance expenses, and accrued taxes and interest. All of these must be factored into your budget before determining your **cost of goods sold**. For example, computers must be replaced or updated from time to time. The cost of replacement is as much a part of the cost of your final interactive game as is the cost of content, labor, and advertising.

> **COST OF GOODS SOLD**
> The total cost required to produce a product that has been sold, excluding general operating expenses. This can be broad or narrow, depending on your costing mechanism.

You probably know what revenue is: any money you take in for your service or product. Expenses, on the other hand, are the costs associated with completing or running the project or business. People new to the business world usually don't realize how much can be deducted as expenses for tax purposes. Your own paycheck is included, but only if your company is incorporated. Pro-rated rent, supplies, utilities, research time, reasonable gifts to people who have assisted you, taxes, interest on loans, and any number of other expenses that your accountant should make you aware of go into the expenses side of the income statement. Get receipts for everything. Be careful, however, not to rack up expenses just because you know that you can deduct them. Even large amounts of revenue can be whittled away quickly through a series of seemingly inconsequential expenses.

ABC MULTIMEDIA CORPORATION
Income Statement for Year Ended December 31, 1999

Revenue:
Gross Sales			$500,000
Less: Sales returns and allowances		$15,000	
Less: Sales discounts		20,000	35,000
Net Sales			$465,000

Cost of Goods Sold:
Merchandise Inventory, January 1, 1999		$10,000	
Purchases	$75,000		
Less: Purchases returns and allowances	2,000		
Net Purchases	$73,000		
Add: Freight	1,000		
Cost of Goods Purchased		$74,000	
Goods Available for Sale		84,000	
Merchandise Inventory, December 31, 1999		30,000	
Cost of goods sold			90,000
Gross Profit from Sales			$411,000

Operating Expenses:
Marketing and Selling Expenses:
Sales Salary Expense	$137,000		
Rent Expense	17,000		
Advertising Expense	67,500		
Freight and Delivery Expense	5,000		
Total Marketing and Selling Expenses		$226,500	

General and Administrative Expenses:
Office Salaries Expense	$45,000		
Rent Expense, Office Space	8,000		
Insurance Expense	10,000		
Depreciation Expense, Office Equipment	25,000		
Total General and Administrative Expenses		88,000	
Total Operating Expenses			314,500
Net Income			$96,500

You should prepare an income statement for your overall business, as well as for each separate project. If you are working on more than one project, allocate costs like rent and supplies among all of them, on a pro-rated basis. If you are just beginning a project that has not yet been sold, you can also have a *projected* income statement based on your estimate of the project's eventual earnings. If you are using this statement for financing, you will need some sort of background research – or such evidence as a contract – to establish what your figures are based upon.

The Balance Sheet

This document is a snapshot picture of the financial position of your business at the close of a particular accounting period. Usually balance sheets are compiled monthly, quarterly, and annually. The balance sheet is broken into three sections: assets, liabilities, and equity (sometimes called the capital account). Assets are what you own including what is owed to you and the value of intangibles such as goodwill and copyrights. Liabilities are what you owe. Equity is the difference between the two and represents the total financial interest of all the owners in the business. The balance sheet is useful to give you an idea of how financially stable you are, and is absolutely necessary if you want to get financing.

ABC MULTIMEDIA CORPORATION
Balance Sheet December 31, 1999

Assets

Current Assets:
Cash		$141,500
Accounts receivable		120,000
Inventory		30,000
Prepaid expenses		7,000
Total Current Assets			$298,500

Fixed Assets:
Computer equipment	$76,000		
Less: Accumulated depreciation	20,000	$56,000	
Office equipment	$50,000		
Less: Accumulated depreciation	5,000	45,000	
Building	$150,000		
Less: Accumulated depreciation	6,000	144,000	
Land		50,000	
Total Fixed Assets			$295,000

Intangible Assets:
Goodwill	$10,000	
Copyright	10,000	
Trademarks	5,000	
Patents	20,000	
Total Intangible Assets		45,000
Total Assets		$638,500

Liabilities

Current Liabilities:
Notes payable/Bank advances	$125,000	
Accounts payable	34,000	
Wages payable	20,000	
Dividends payable	5,000	
Income taxes payable	10,000	
Total Current Liabilities		$250,000

Long-Term Liabilities:
Mortgage payable		144,000
Total Liabilities		$394,000

Shareholder Equity

Capital Stock	$100,000	
Contributed surplus	44,500	
Retained earnings	100,000	
Total Equity		244,500
Total Liabilities and Equity		$638,500

Take a look at the sample balance sheet on page 70. Nearly every balance sheet you are likely to see will follow the same general format. Accountants have set up a uniform system of accounting called **Generally Accepted Accounting Principles (GAAP)** to guide the way all financial matters are dealt with. Keeping the format the same allows for a proper comparison of companies, and helps to prevent companies from hiding discrepancies from investors or the government.

> **GENERALLY ACCEPTED ACCOUNTING PRINCIPLES (GAAP)**
> The specific rules and common practices to be used in general accounting as set out by the institutes of accountants in various jurisdictions. These include the rules under which financial statements are prepared.

You will notice that the two totals in the balance sheet are equal. You guessed it: that's why they call it a *balance* sheet. The items in the balance sheet should be listed in a particular order, from the most liquid to the least liquid (i.e., most easily converted to cash). Current assets and liabilities are those that are available or due within the present year. Be aware that you cannot make up or approximate any of these numbers. Some bankers or investors will require the balance sheet – and all financial statements – to be audited by an accountant. If you are using statements that have not been audited, be prepared to show extensive evidence of how you arrived at your figures. Even with such evidence, many financial institutions will require that the statements be audited before any investment moneys are actually advanced.

The Statement of Retained Earnings

The amount left in the business after any dividends have been paid to investors (including yourself) is summarized in the statement of retained earnings. Retained earnings are important because they represent your ability to plan for the future. It's often useful to combine the income statement and the statement of retained earnings to show the complete history of your business for the year.

ABC MULTIMEDIA CORPORATION
Statement of Retained Earnings
for Year Ended December 31, 1999

Balance at beginning of year...............................	$8,500	
Net earnings for the year.......................................	96,500	
Available for dividend disbursement		$105,000
Deduct: Dividends (payments to owners)		5,000
Balance at end of year		$100,000

The Statement of Changes in Financial Position

This statement shows how you obtained cash and what you have done with it. It compares this year's results with those of last year. Investors want to see this statement as an analytical tool to determine if your company is becoming more profitable, spending less in interest payments, or earning a higher net income. You can use this statement to analyze how well your company performed in three general categories: operating activities, financing activities, and investment activities.

ABC MULTIMEDIA CORPORATION
Statement of Changes in Financial Position for Year Ended December 31, 1999

	1999	1998
Operating Activities:		
Net earnings for the period	$96,500	$50,000
Add: items not involving cash:		
Depreciation and amortization	25,000	20,000
Net change in non-cash operating items	25,000	20,000
	146,500	90,000
Financing Activities:		
Repayment of old long-term debt	(20,000)	(18,000)
Borrowing of new long-term debt	0	88,000
Dividends paid (payments to owners)	(5,000)	(5,000)
	(25,000)	65,000
Investing Activities:		
Purchase of fixed assets	(50,000)	(100,000)
Proceeds from sale of fixed assets	0	10,000
	(50,000)	(90,000)
Increase (decrease) in cash	71,500	65,000
Cash beginning of year	70,000	5,000
Cash end of year	$141,500	$70,000

Reading Financial Statements

On first glance, there are some obvious points that you should notice and consider. You want assets to be high and liabilities to be low in the balance sheet. If net income is low, look at the individual elements of the income statement. Are you paying too much to produce, sell, or manage? If retained earnings decreased this year, find out where you spent money in comparison with the previous year. If possible, compare your statements to those of similar companies. Some financial statements are only useful for comparison – either to previous years' activities or to a competitor.

If you're thinking about investing in a multimedia company, beware the tricks that make its financial position appear better than it really is. In traditional businesses, a million dollars in assets can secure a million-dollar loan because if the business fails or the loan is not repaid, the security can be seized and sold to pay back the investor. In multimedia companies, most tangible assets are computers, software, and related equipment. That means the assets worth a million dollars may become obsolete in a few months. At the very least, these assets will have decreased in value in a much shorter time that most other security assets. Investors should be cautious of the company that doesn't accurately depreciate capital goods. Make sure that any investment you make is covered by assets that will retain their value for the entire period of your investment, such as land, buildings, or valuable office furnishings. As well, some equipment depreciates more slowly, such as video cameras, for example. These assets must also be marketable. Before investing, consider the possibility that the company might fail leaving you stuck with a customized retail location and stock you can't sell. Developers looking for financing should recognize that investors notice these creative accounting practices.

There are other financial statements your accountant can outline which may be useful for your particular type of business. The elements from the financial statements are widely used in comparison with each other by financial analysts, investors, and creditors. The results are called ratios, and they are used to compare your business to other similar or comparable businesses.

Ratios

If you don't keep in line with other comparable businesses, you will be seen as a bad investment, a bad credit risk and, ultimately, a company to avoid. Your financial statements should be accompanied by a full set of notes and explanations detailing the reasons for any figures that do not conform to industry norms. Investors should use these figures to calculate ratios to compare your business with others. Such ratios as **debt to equity** and the **acid test** give those outside your company a general picture of your liquidity, profitability, operations activity, and leverage capacity.

DEBT/EQUITY RATIO
This ratio can show if a company is borrowing excessively.

ACID TEST
Also called the quick ratio, the acid test is a stringent measure of corporate liquidity. It shows how well a company can cover its debts by dividing current liability by current assets.

Liquidity ratios show a company's ability to meet its short-term debts by comparing current assets to current liabilities. This is important for debt holders and investors who want to ensure that the company can cover its operating costs.

Profitability ratios show how effective the company, and management in particular, has been in its production and sales activities. The profit margin shows the relationship of income to sales. The operating profit margin takes away all revenues from peripheral sources such as investments and interest. That way you can better understand how effective the company has been in actual operations. Profitability ratios usually measure a company's profit in relation to sales, total assets, and owner's equity.

Operations activity ratios show turnover of inventory, fixed assets, operating assets, and total assets. Inventory turnover is the most frequently used operations activity ratio, since it shows how often or how quickly you are able to sell your products. Unlike food, multimedia products are not perishable so they will not physically spoil if they are not sold within a particular time period. Many multimedia products are used for reference, so they are filled with information or other content that becomes obsolete or out of fashion after a period of time. The amount of time your product will retain its value should be explained in detail in the notes accompanying your financial analysis. If the content in your product will not become obsolete, this is an important benefit and should be stressed.

Ratios for leverage capacity show how your company is financed in relation to assets, equity, and debt. They show how well your company is covered in terms of interest payments and dividend payments. These are important because your company's leverage capacity allows you to plan for the future.

Don't get bogged down with keeping to a particular ratio if you are just beginning to develop your business. No company starts out as a financial star. A multimedia company may need to go through long periods of high debt before it starts to show a real profit. The important thing is to ensure that your company is *increasingly* profitable.

TRENDS

It is important to compare your present financial position with your position over the past few years. To do this financial people use trend lines. Most comparisons use only the past five years. For example, take your cash flow ratio figure from five years ago as your base. The trend figure for that year is 100%. Divide the ratio figures for each of the next years by this base to find four new percentages. What investors (or potential clients) look for is a steadily improving trend.

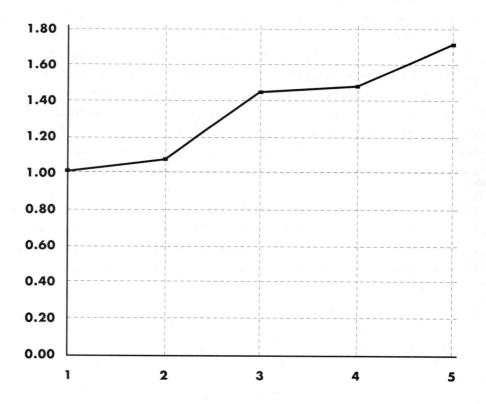

If you haven't been in business for five years, just make a trend line for the figures you have. If there has been a material change in the business in any of the years being analyzed, explain it. Few investors will avoid your company simply because there was a glitch in the trend line one year. As long as you can show that your company has recovered strongly and you can explain the reason for the glitch, your company will still appear viable. The multimedia industry is rapidly evolving, so periodic refocusing of the business, investing in hot new hardware, and even absorbing new business partners into your company may be a regular occurrence. Any of these business decisions may cause a dip in the trend line.

Depreciation

We have already mentioned the significance of depreciation to a multimedia company. You should also know how to account for depreciation. First you should know that land does not depreciate. Any increase or decrease in its value is only counted in the year that it is sold or otherwise disposed. Operating equipment *does* depreciate. Computers, scanners, and other equipment become obsolete or simply wear out. You are permitted to deduct part of the original cost of the equipment every year for tax purposes. Even though computers and related technology become obsolete quickly for multimedia companies, many tax laws restrict depreciation of such technology.

There are many methods of depreciation, with the most common being the straight-line method. To use this, estimate the **salvage value** of a particular piece of equipment and deduct this from the original cost. Divide the result by the estimated number of years the equipment will be used by the company. This is the amount that can be deducted for each of those years. Your accountant may recommend other methods of depreciation that suit your situation. The choice of a depreciation method is often dictated by your tax laws peculiar to your case. Whichever depreciation method you use,

SALVAGE VALUE
The amount you can get for a piece of operating equipment after your business is finished using it.

you have to be consistent for tax purposes. You can't frequently change methods for tax accounting, although the way you value your assets in your non-tax corporate books is up to you. Tax inspectors will take a close look at your company if they suspect you are playing fast and loose with your tax accounting.

Taxes, Permits, and Licensing

Taxes are the bane of any entrepreneur. As much as you'd like to concentrate on running the business, you must also spend time completing government forms and making tax payments. There are business taxes, real estate taxes, sales taxes, excise taxes, federal taxes, state or provincial taxes, county or regional taxes, city or municipal taxes, goods and services taxes, value-added taxes, and any number of other taxes that cannot be avoided. Some of these must be paid whether or not any income is generated. The time required for accounting and filing tax returns is another cost of doing business. Added to these costs and hassles is the filing of information statements – often incurring an annual filing fee.

A variety of different government departments want to know what you are doing, and you have little choice but to tell them. Know what you are getting into from the beginning. Talk to your accountant and lawyer to get a precise list of the taxes and other requirements you will have to deal with in your jurisdiction.

How to Talk with Your Banker or Venture Capitalist

Bankers and other investors are in business to make money for their companies or for themselves. Don't go into a long speech on how your company can help the world communicate. Tell them how your company will make money. Tell them how long it will take to return a profit, the risks involved, and the potential amount of profit. Show them that you know and have what it takes to make money.

Introduction to Finance

One last point: appearance is key. Bankers and venture capitalists have a short period of time to size you up, and how you look is part of your overall assessment. You should wear a suit in traditional business colors. Men should wear a conservative tie. Times may be changing the face and spirit of the multimedia world, but bankers and others in the financial industry have remained conservative. Although there are cultural differences depending on your geography, it is always better to over-dress than to under-dress. Consider this the most important job interview of your life. Without money, you can't start (or continue) your project. One exception to the dress code might be in Silicon Valley where a laid-back style is the rule. Even there, however, bankers wear suits.

Why not scope out the bank or other institution before you go in for a loan?

Chapter 7

Distribution — How to Get Your Product to Your Customers

Introduction to Distribution

In Chapter 5, we talked about selling your multimedia product. This chapter deals with the process by which your finished products get into your customers' hands. Distribution refers to the long chain of events that exchanges your finished product for cash. Depending on the product, this process can take days, weeks, or even months. Generally, physically large or big-ticket items are sold through distributors. Most computer systems, printers, and other related gear, are *moved* from the vendor through the distributor to your neighborhood stores. Smaller products such as CD-ROMs and software are often available in the same way. However, these products are also available through mail-order catalogs and other channels like direct-to-the-customer advertising. Sometimes they are exclusively available through these direct channels. This way of skipping the retail level is called "going direct." To go direct, the vendor either becomes the distributor or uses a clearing house for distribution.

There are reasons for going direct and reasons for using a distributor. We will present the pros and cons of each, outlining why skipping a layer and going direct is sometimes a masterful stroke of brilliant marketing and in other situations can ruin your business. We'll also show you how to go about setting up the best distribution network for your product.

In the early days of CD-ROMs, relationships among the developer, the publisher, and the distributor were well defined. The developer worked strictly on implementing an idea or concept using programming languages and other tools. The developer's purpose was to produce multimedia titles. The publisher concentrated its efforts on bringing CD-ROM titles to market. This focus included designing the packaging, arranging for and signing the legal agreement with a third-party distribution company (or companies), and even placing advertising to generate customer demand. Finally, the distributor took the final, published product and sold it to retail stores.

Today, there is an increasing blurring of the roles between publishers and distributors. Many CD-ROM developers have started to publish their discs independently in a process called, understandably, self-publishing. These hybrid developers/publishers often publish their own titles and those of other, smaller developers as well.

Consult Chapter 15 for a list of mail order houses.

Mail order is an interesting avenue to investigate if you intend to self-publish your title. In mail order, the catalog is your product's showroom and your product's description is your salesperson. With the proliferation of mail order opportunities and other direct sales channels, the line between CD-ROM publishing and distribution has become even more blurred. We talk more about mail order later in this chapter.

If they do not choose the self-publishing option, developers still sign agreements with publishers and distributors. Publishing agreements are typically exclusive. That is, you as the developer, can sign with only one publisher for a particular title. Since you are bound by the exclusive nature of your contract, be careful and make sure you understand all that you are getting into beforehand.

Distribution agreements, on the other hand, may or may not be exclusive. Certain distribution houses require that a title be distributed *only* by them. Many affiliate label programs, for instance, often try to tie up developers in exclusive deals for a certain period of time or for a certain number of titles. We discuss affiliate label programs in greater detail later in this chapter. However developers can often obtain non-exclusive agreements with distribution companies – especially niche or regional distributors.

Let's see how a decision to publish your CD-ROM can affect your distribution options.

Three Publishing Options

If you are producing CD-ROMs or other mass-distributed multimedia products, the three publishing options you have are using an established publisher, using an affiliate label, or self-publishing.

You have the least control over your work if you sell your completed content lock, stock, and barrel to a publisher. An established publisher produces the finished work, handles duplication, packaging, advertising, distribution, and sales. For you to make money in this type of deal, your publishers must be well-connected, well-organized, and capable. You will not receive as high a royalty percentage for your work in comparison to self-publishing your disc, but you will not have to pay the costs of distribution either. You may get a flat fee, or a small royalty percentage of perhaps 15 percent (or less) of the wholesale price. In other situations, you may be able to negotiate a combination of an advance and a royalty.

Three Publishing Options

	SELF-PUBLISHING	AFFILIATE LABEL	ESTABLISHED PUBLISHER
Up-front payment to developer	$0	$0	$0 – $millions [1]
Royalties	100%	Usually between 50 and 70% (in favor of the publisher).	0 – 40% [1]
Distribution costs	100%	0%	0%
Distribution scope	Usually limited, especially for small companies.	Relatively wide, depending on label.	Usually wide, often with entire country continent coverage.
Barriers to entry	Money for packaging, design, collateral promotion, etc.	Existing product with some sales, or a name in the industry.	Difficult – generally needs at least one previous successful product.

[1] Established or famous content providers (like Peter Gabriel or David Bowie) can command extremely high signing inducements. Beginning developers will have little or no leverage and may get no up-front money and a low royalty percentage.

Multimedia publishers are typically difficult to pin down where royalties, advances, and margins are concerned. This is due to competitive pressures – for example, the Voyager Company doesn't want Sony Electronic Publishing to know what it is paying its developers, and it doesn't want one developer to know how much another gets. In addition, royalties, advances, and payouts vary by many factors, including celebrity endorsements, packaging, track record, and expected demand. A CD-ROM title about the Olympics may sell well just before and during the Games, but will likely decrease in value soon after the closing ceremonies.

Check out Chapter 15 for a list of multimedia publishers, distributors, and developers.

If you wish to take more control of your product but you do not have the bandwidth, contacts, or support system to take publishing and distribution in-house, you may opt for an affiliate label program. Under this program you produce the finished work, handle the disc duplication, manual writing and printing and sometimes even the final packaging and marketing. You sign over exclusive publishing rights to your product to a more established publishing company. The theory is, by signing over your exclusive rights, you receive greater marketing push from an established company. This in turn should give your product access to a large market. The down side is that these established companies typically have many other titles that they also wish to sell. But just because you have signed with a well-known label, don't think you can relax and wait for the money to come rolling in. Different affiliate labels have different policies regarding the residual rights of their developers – so it pays to ask (and get it in writing). In the final analysis — even if you have a program encompassing marketing activities — generating a marketing push always remains your responsibility. You might get a higher local profile with a smaller regional distribution house. These smaller companies will give you more attention but, due to their smaller size and weaker market strength, your overall exposure will be smaller. Your choice is between marketing push and marketing bandwidth. Big or small, the informed decision is yours.

If you choose self-publishing you are responsible for the entire deal. This includes production, duplication, packaging, marketing, advertising, distribution, sales, fulfillment, and everything else. You have complete control over your product, but with control come responsibilities and costs. If you have lots of sales and marketing experience in the computer and consumer packaged goods industries, go for it. Otherwise, seriously consider using an affiliate label or a traditional publisher to get your title on the retailers' shelf.

People new to business sometimes think that distribution just deals with the decision to sell products using mail order or retail. In fact, this is just the tip of the iceberg. What you must decide is how you want to run your business. How far do you want to be "dug in"? Do you want to set up an entire company department whose sole responsibility is packaging, taking orders, fulfilling orders, and generally dealing with customer demands? Or do you want to concern yourself solely with the creative aspects of the project, and have someone else deal with the hassle of packaging and distribution? Does your answer change if you have to work through a major publishing house and give up control of how the product will be packaged and shown to your audience? You may wish to take gradual control by using third-party fulfillment houses for your first few products, and then move all distribution activities in-house. On the other hand, using a single major distributor may work for the life of your company if you can find one that will represent your products and company favorably and not take an excessive margin. Shop around before you sign on with any distributor.

Costs of Distribution

In distribution, you get what you pay for. Distributors don't work for free – and whoever eventually collects the profits also pays the piper. Even if you decide to self-publish, you will not work entirely alone.

We will not go into detail about production and mastering costs, but they should be considered in your decision as well. Replication of CD-ROM discs in bulk can usually be obtained for about US$1 per disc, or less. Depending on the size of the run, the manufacturing plant may also reduce the cost of the glass mastering process to zero when you replicate your discs with them. Some established CD-ROM replication companies will waive the glass-mastering if you order thousands of discs. The down side is that you might have to replicate more discs than you would have otherwise wanted, thus tying up your money. In other words, you end up paying one way or the other. Anyway, manufacturing the final product is only a small portion of the costs involved.

Packaging design is a major part of your marketing strategy. At the retail level, packaging can make or break the sale. Your design, therefore, should be determined by those experienced in product marketing. You might wonder why we're talking about packaging in the distribution

DIMENSIONALITY

Look and feel of a multimedia product in its retail packaging. It should aid your marketing efforts by sticking out to retail purchasers, by being recognizable, and possibly by influencing a buying decision.

section of the book. The reason is that packaging your product and preparing it for final sale is key to distribution. If a product is being sold retail, success depends on **dimensionality** and the wow factor. On the other hand, if a product is being sold through catalog mail order, a catchy title and compelling advertising blurb may be all prospective customers see. Find a design and stick with it for any subsequent products. By having a similar look and feel for every product at the retail level, you start developing brand awareness and loyalty from your customers. When you are designing your packaging, keep in mind that your product may be sold in other retail establishments such as traditional bookstores and even audio and video stores.

If you use an established distributor, this company will absorb a sizable percentage of your gross profit. It may be worth the price since the distributor will be responsible for all the costs of distribution including shipping to resellers. Besides, a distribution company is more likely to get your product into big-name or specialty retail outlets since it has the appropriate contacts. If a distributor is handling mail order for you, you won't have to deal with all the nagging details – toll-free numbers, credit card orders, returns, customer service, and freight. Although mail order is mostly a North American phenomenon, it is starting to catch on in other countries

OPPORTUNITY COST

The option you give up when you choose to do something else.

as well. The bottom line is that the **opportunity cost** of dealing with distribution yourself is the lost time you could have spent on production and development.

Outsourcing your distribution may be your best solution unless you are extremely knowledgeable and experienced in the field. Stick to what you do best. If you are a code jockey or content developer, your time is probably most profitably spent in production, not distribution. Many multimedia producers incorrectly assume that major expenses will be incurred if they use a distribution or fulfillment company to move their products. It really means you receive less money per package or title, *but* – and this better be true if your distribution company is worth its salt – your sales volume will greatly increase along with your profits.

These days you cannot expect customers to pay for their long-distance calls to order your products. Just about everyone in North America uses toll-free numbers, so if you want to sell your product direct you will need to get one. Customers calling to order will want to pay with a credit card, so you have to do credit card authorizations as well. The cost of credit card authorization is between 1.5 percent and 5 percent of the total order in North America. This percentage depends on the price of the typical product you sell as well as your overall volume. In general, you'll get better (i.e., lower) rates for a higher priced product with high volume sales. As well, you generally need a clear credit record yourself and a confirmed financial plan, which the credit card company will want to see. Finally, you will generally have to provide a security deposit of about 10 percent of sales for your first month and an additional small percentage of sales for refunds. You have to accept credit cards if you sell direct, so make the best deal you can, and you should aim at securing a 2 percent (or lower) authorization fee.

Good distributors frequently offer sales discounts and allowances for those willing to pay cash to avoid the payment delay. In practice, no one in the computer, entertainment, or multimedia industries pays cash for anything. However, it's always nice to have cash, so the cash discount offer has become standard.

If you are self-publishing, wastage can be expensive. If, for instance, your inlay cards are printed with an unauthorized logo, an inverted title, or some other error, the entire job will have to be scrapped and redone. Another worry in the distribution and sales cycle is shrinkage. In business, shrinkage refers to spoilage, shop-lifting, or other reduction of your inventory due to unplanned circumstances. If you're selling your multimedia product in retail stores, you probably don't have to worry about shop-lifting or other forms of customer-related shrinkage. Most of the time, the distributor or retailer absorbs the financial loss that shrinkage brings. The major exception is when you place your products in a retail store on consignment.

Offering your products on consignment is not a suggested long-term plan, but may be very effective in the short-run. You can talk directly to the owner or manager of a computer shop, a bookstore, or other retail outlet. Offer them a percentage of the profits if they are willing to carry your product in their store. Managers of large chain stores generally won't have the authority to accept such an arrangement unless the store is manager-owned. The more autonomy they have, the better for you. Consignment offers you the chance to test your product on the open market without having to commit to mass production. If the product sells well, you have revenue with which to produce more of your product. If it doesn't, you haven't blown all your chances with the big national distributors. At any rate, you gain valuable feedback to help you improve your product. Besides, if it sells you have a successful commodity with a track record. You can then take your product to a major distribution house with evidence of profitability.

Even the best product is periodically returned by a dissatisfied customer. Multimedia sales differ from most other product sales in that returns are not usually allowed for mere product dissatisfaction. Software vendors generally have a policy disallowing returns after the seal on the packaging has been broken. This prevents would-be pirates from copying the discs and then claiming a refund because of dissatisfaction. This policy does not apply if the product is defective in any way. One way to stimulate sales may be to offer a no-questions-asked-money-back guarantee. This allows purchasers to return the product if they choose to do so. In practice, a very low percentage of people actually take advantage of this option. However, you still have to deal with returns and potential piracy from the ones that do. Returns can also cause an administrative nightmare for your customer service and accounting departments.

As we mentioned in Chapter 6, software developers must deal with product wastage caused by periodic upgrades. All products on the shelf are pulled to make way for the new versions. This leaves possibly thousands of copies wasted or requiring further costly changes before they can be sold. If yours is the kind of product that changes from period to period through upgrades, then this wastage must be included in your budget forecasting. Some enterprising companies have created alternate channels to distribute their older, otherwise obsolete, products. Such methods include alternate market sales (for example, to emerging European countries), hardware bundling, and even trade-show giveaways. Many multimedia products, such as games, are time-resistant. If, however, your product is an atlas, encyclopedia, almanac, or other reference material, you should factor in this periodic updating into your initial budget.

A major concern and cost for mail order catalog sales is fulfillment. This part of the distribution chain includes handling orders, administration, and delivery. Naturally, all these distribution elements have costs associated with them, and the more you sell the lower your cost per order. The costs associated with ordering are toll-free line charges, staff to handle the calls, and an order entry system to keep track of the orders. Administration requirements include the tabulation of orders, organization of stock and warehousing, and database management for customer tracking. The costs of delivery are freight, handling, and postage or courier charges. Some of these costs may be added to the sales price of the product, but you still have to absorb some administration charges associated with the delivery process.

Fulfillment Companies

Making it easy for your prospect to buy from you is the name of the sales game. This is especially important for small companies. Fulfillment companies represent a quick and painless way for your customers to order from you. Almost equally important, they make your company appear bigger than it actually is. Some fulfillment companies operate 24 hours a day, seven days a week – others run on a more traditional 9 a.m. to 5 p.m. schedule. Most fulfillment companies accept all major credit cards for billing purposes. Furthermore, some of these companies can have your customers' cash in your bank account within a few hours.

Other companies are experimenting with using the local telephone company to collect the money for an order. In North America, for example, the 1-900 and 1-976 services are being used to sell consumer products. Instead of charging by the minute, a set charge is made for a specific product and automatically appears on your customer's monthly phone bill. This creative way of selling overcomes credit problems as people do not need a credit card to order. The down side is that unscrupulous customers try to convince the telephone company they never ordered or received your product and refuse to pay. As you can see, this sales method might be best suited for moving low-cost items or samples. For these products, it won't bankrupt your business if you have to write off a few bad debts.

As we've mentioned throughout this book, your business will change over time. Successful multimedia companies might go through four (or more) phases of distribution before settling on the most viable solution. In the first phase, most developers do all their distribution themselves on a strictly local basis. This means they might start off by selling a few dozen CD-ROMs, for example, at a local trade show. Soon they are able to sell their disc through a small distributor and gain additional customers and a small market share. Strengthened by these encouraging beginnings as well as new business contacts, they begin to take more control over the distribution of their products.

In the third phase, the company uses a third-party fulfillment company to distribute a product they have mastered, duplicated, and packaged themselves. Finally, the company may begin to resent the large amount of money a fulfillment company charges, so they create an in-house distribution mechanism. In the world of distribution, every small company has to learn how to walk before it runs but it helps to have a map to prevent you from getting lost.

Understanding North American Distribution Realities

Distribution in North America is clearly dominated by the three main distributors of computer-related products: Ingram, Merisel, and Tech Data in order of size. They play a middle role between customers and computer and software manufacturers. Both Merisel and Ingram currently have over 20,000 products on their price lists and Tech Data has upward of 10,000.

Check out Chapter 15 for distribution companies.

Faced with these numbers, how can you hope to be stand out from the competition? No matter who you are, you will get lost in the mountains of other titles, tools, or multimedia services. Larger and more established companies like Lotus Development, for example, can sometimes negotiate a deal with the distributor to run special promotions and bundles. But what if you don't have a multimillion-dollar advertising budget that is capable of enticing customers into the stores? What then? Then, you get creative.

Maybe using one of the big three distributors isn't best for you. There are a variety of options available to you. Using a medium-sized distributor specializing in CD-ROM products, like Baker & Taylor for example, may be a better first distribution choice. Perhaps a smaller, lesser-known distributor can do a better job for you. Compare catalogs from the big three with those of small distributors. Think about how your product matches the business model of each company. Do any of these distributors understand *your* market? Perhaps the best way for you to proceed is to use a few small distributors in the early stages and approach a large distributor when you have established name recognition.

Every distributor will want to feel comfortable with your product. The distributor knows the cold, hard truth about the market. If your product is a children's disc entitled *Learning Fractions* with a Spanish translation built in, tell the distributor how the translation feature will increase market penetration. If, however, your U.S.-targeted business title has a similar second language capacity, don't mention it. English is the language of business in North America; so distributors want to see business CD-ROMs in English only. By presenting a bilingual English-Spanish business CD-ROM title you might be telling your national distributor you don't have a clear focus on your market. Of course, if your market expects your title to be bilingual, then by all means promote this feature as a benefit.

Regional distributors, especially in the southern areas of Florida, Texas, and California, may have a different opinion about your English/Spanish business disc. These distributors are targeted in their marketing strategies and know who to approach. Just because a company is large doesn't mean it has the answers to everyone's needs. After all, a certain worldwide fast food chain sells over 28 million meals every day. It doesn't mean the food is gourmet and it *certainly* doesn't mean you should even think about distributing through them if you're marketing a Dining Out CD-ROM. When you start negotiating with distribution houses, think about distribution and cross-promotion proposals of your own. Use your distributor's size to leverage yourself in the marketplace.

It's getting easier for small multimedia production houses to enter the market. One-off CD-ROM machines have become inexpensive, and replication services and color copiers are at many corner stores. As more basement operations are getting it together and producing their first title, other markets in Europe, the Pacific Rim, and Australia are now emerging as multimedia powerhouses. The rapid increase in CD-ROM drive penetration is revolutionizing the worldwide multimedia industry.

Unless your product really is the best thing since the floppy disk, and you have a fortune to invest on supplementary marketing, it's probably best to stay away from the national distributors at first. Even regional distributors, if they are large enough, have the bandwidth and marketing strength to do what they please with your product. Smaller focused distributors may do more for you even though it doesn't feed your ego as would listing with the Big Three.

Try not to sign exclusive distribution agreements with any third-party distribution company unless you go with a national distributor. Perhaps a few smaller companies in different markets or regions will end up selling far more of your products than would one large distributor.

What Distributors Look for in a New Product

Distributors want to see a potentially high-volume product and a successful, well-organized company behind it. National distributors – such as Merisel or Ingram – will want to see a finished product before they will even talk to you. Their reality is that they cannot afford to spend time on a product that may never see the light of day. However if you are approaching a regional or local distributor, the product may not need to be completed to secure a tentative distribution agreement. You can impress regional or local distributors with a prototype, a detailed business plan and market research. The prototype should have at least one section that is completed, and all of the interactive elements within this section should be fully functional.

Don't spend too much money on an initial prototype if you know you will need to obtain financing or go into a joint venture. The other party will likely require significant input that could drastically change the work you would have already put into a prototype. No matter which level of distributor you approach, your relationship with a distributor can be used to leverage your position with venture capitalists or investors.

A distributor will feel more confident about you and your product if either one has a good track record. If your product sold out in a week when you put it in a store on consignment, the distributor should know this. Bring testimonials to support your claim in the form of letters from store managers or any press coverage your product receives. If you were once a corporate marketing manager, provide a list of your successes. Show how your market insight resulted in your company doubling its sales, for example. As long as these are transferable skills, your distributor is more likely to believe you're capable of reading the market and creating a customer demand for the product. A product produced by a good marketer is more likely to sell.

A distributor knows that packaging is a major factor in selling the product, especially at the retail level. Have on hand design samples and a complete understanding of the costs related to packaging. At the retail level, packaging is a significant cost of your product. (One of the reasons you can discount your product so much when bundling is that the fancy retail packaging expense is eliminated.) For a retail CD-ROM title, for instance, US$5 or $6 is the maximum you should be spending for the entire cost of goods sold. This includes the cost of the disc itself, the liner card, the manual in the form of inlay notes, the jewel case, shrink-wrapping, and stickering at the retail level. Certain major publishers produce CD-ROM packages that include a two-panel fold-over pack, liner notes, and the CD-ROM itself for between US$1.50 and US$3, depending upon the quantity.

The designers creating your packaging should know to include a Universal Product Code (UPC) sequence on the outside of your product. As well, you should work with retailers to create checkout-friendly packaging. You may consider these points minor or irrelevant in comparison to the development of the actual product. The fact is, the details are what give you the edge over your competition. Checkout-friendly packaging shows distributors and retailers that you understand the cold, hard realities of sales and distribution. They will appreciate you putting yourself in their shoes. The result should be a long-term sales relationship. **Racking** and other point-of-sale merchandising devices should also be discussed with your distributor.

RACKING
Devices used in a store to showcase your product.

APPROACHING DISTRIBUTORS

In a way, approaching a distributor is a lot like approaching a venture capital firm. Before most venture capital companies will touch a first-time producer, they must see a distribution contract for the product. Similarly, few distributors will agree to carry a product unless it is at least close to completion and is well-financed. In some ways, distribution companies work like the venture capitalist companies that we talked about earlier in the book. Associates in VC companies are usually expected to examine over 100 proposals every month. This means that, in addition to their other responsibilities, they look through more than five proposals each day, every day. Even large VC firms take only five major deals to market in a year. The biggest firms might do a few more than five but would never consider any more than 10 in a given year.

The odds of your product getting picked up by a distributor are a bit better than this – but not much better. Many first-time multimedia producers are frustrated by this marketing reality. Distributors know that their assistance can make or break a product. However, they also know that there are many distributors you can approach. Distributors are highly competitive for products they believe will sell. Just like the VC people, however, distributors are approached every day by hundreds of wannabe producers. Even though distributors don't make the same financial commitment as would a VC firm, they still don't have time to waste. If you have a story to tell, tell it well, but tell it quickly. Make it easy for them to say "Yes."

DISTRIBUTOR PRODUCT REVIEW PROCESS

The key management staff at distribution companies typically have weekly meetings to discuss and review potential new product that have been sent by prospective vendors or simply purchased from computer stores. Due to the volume of products sent in for review, they have very little time to make decisions. The bad news is you only get about five minutes to sell your product. The worse news is you aren't here to do the selling. That means you need a compelling story that will jump out at the distributor. An innovative marketing teaser, striking package artwork, and a ready market all factor into the decision to carry your product.

A "leave behind" that defines your product, its target market and hardware platforms, followed by a page of points describing your marketing budget and plan, is also useful. Make certain that *all* your information sheets have contact names and telephone numbers.

Incredibly, even surviving the rigorous selection process is no guarantee of success. Have a look at the pages of Redwood City, California-based *Red Herring* or Toronto, Ontario-based *Media Access Report*. Both these publications outline recent successes and failures in the high-tech world. Many VC-backed firms – ones with good, solid distribution contracts as well – never make it to the second round of financing.

Bundling

The philosophy behind bundling is that, by combining forces, complementary vendors can offer an entire solution to a specific customer set. These vendors offer their products at significant discounts in exchange for the extra market share (or royalty) and promotional value of appearing in a bundle. There is often a name recognition factor at play. Historically, small producers appear more successful when their product is sold in conjunction with a big-name hardware vendor. The small producer gains marketing clout through this inclusion that helps it in future marketing efforts.

Major hardware and software manufacturers look upon bundling as a great way to expand their market share at a relatively low cost. Bundling deals are typically organized between complementary products and similar markets. For instance, if you have a clip art CD-ROM, you might choose to bundle your product with a business presentation software vendor and a CD-ROM drive manufacturer. In this example, as with all successful bundling deals, none of the manufacturers is in competition with each other. In fact, each vendor promotes the other indirectly. By bundling, you hope to market the entire package as having added value as a benefit to your customer.

Types of Bundles

As multimedia spreads into more and more markets, the types of bundles become more diverse. Past examples of multimedia bundles include multimedia authoring solutions, video editing solutions, desktop publishing packages, home office packages, and optical character recognition packages. **Vertical market** bundling holds great opportunities for specific sets of customers. The good thing about customers in these vertical markets is that they tend to have more money than most customers. In addition, they tend to be more receptive to a bundle than traditional customers. The bad thing about vertical markets is that they are extremely focused and they can be small.

> **VERTICAL MARKET**
> A market with a clearly defined vocation, such as dentists or architects. Compare with horizontal market with a much broader base.

If you have a consumer or retail title, you may want to contact hardware developers who have specific consumer-oriented computer models on the market. Apple USA, for example, markets the Macintosh Performa computer series. These computers are pre-loaded with specific software packages that vary depending on the market. It's hard to break into these bundles. However, if your product adds considerably more value than it costs, you may have a chance. Before you knock on any door, consider how your product can add value, thereby helping the hardware developer market the entire bundle.

How to Get into a Bundle

The dream of many small multimedia producers is to have their product become part of a bundle. We are approached regularly to provide assistance in making this happen. We suggest you start by contacting the marketing manager for the major (i.e., anchor) product in the bundle. The anchor product generally has a relatively large sticker price to allow for some opportunity to hide the cost of *your* product in the bundle. Computer systems, large peripherals, and expensive software packages are all examples of a bundle anchor. Suggest a deal to the marketing manager whereby he or she would purchase your product at a significant discount in exchange for adding value to his or her customers.

Obviously, you have a much better bargaining position if you already have a name established for yourself in the marketplace. Be prepared to deal. If your retail product has a suggested retail price (SRP, in retailing parlance) of $99.95, its street price is likely around $80. The anchor bundling partner won't be interested in including your product unless your price is certainly under $10, maybe even $5 – or less. This leads us nicely to the next section – bundling tradeoffs.

Bundling Tradeoffs – Revenue vs. Exposure

If you're happily selling your product for a wholesale price of $55 and the computer stores are selling it for a street price of $80, why would you possibly consider selling it for $10 (or less)? At that price, what's in it for you? Good question. There are many reasons to bundle a product at, or slightly above, cost. The first two reasons are to increase volume and grab more market share. By increasing volume through this bundle you may be able to achieve better efficiencies of production. You may go into the next discount level for disc replication, for example, and be able to reduce your wholesale or retail prices. By increasing your market share you actually make it to an editor's in-box and grab more attention in his or her "what's happening" column. As long as you break even or make a little money you're ahead of the game.

Some manufacturers offer developers royalty deals. These are ventures where the manufacturer handles all replication, packaging, and distribution for the bundle. The developer is paid US$1 or US$2 per disc but has no costs to bear. This is especially attractive to a developer if the title is nearly or already dead on the market, if you can convince the bundle manufacturer to take your product.

One note of caution however: be careful not to cannibalize your existing retail channel with your bundling efforts. By cannibalize we mean replacing full-price retail sales with low-margin original equipment manufacturer (OEM) sales. Don't bundle your one and only product unless you are going to make millions tagging along in the bundle.

Bundling is particularly attractive if you have an older version of software or a new CD-ROM title coming on the market soon. In either of these cases, market cannibalization doesn't much matter if your bundled product is at the end of its useful life anyway. Use the bundled product to build sales of the new product. Include demos of the new product with the older product if possible. Also be aware that some unscrupulous computer store managers frequently unbundle your product, sell each product in their store at the full retail price, and pocket the difference. These people hurt everyone in the long run.

Bundling is attractive to small multimedia developers for a number of different reasons. To be successful in bundling, however, you have to keep your product costs down. One way to do this is the accepted practice of minimizing retail packaging for an OEM product. By reducing the amount of packaging, you save costs as well as help prevent any attempts at unbundling described in the previous section. Don't worry about losing the sale because your product isn't all dressed up in its finery. It's this finery that makes many CD-ROM discs expensive. Your bundled product is already sold – don't worry about how it looks. Worry, rather, that you've included enough marketing material in the packaging to drive sales of another, more profitable product.

You may want to consider registration cards. Registration cards are an invaluable method to keep in touch with your customers. Unfortunately, many customers fail to return the completed cards to the software vendor or hardware manufacturer. Return rates of such cards for computer systems, for example, run at about 60 percent or less. Software registration cards enjoy a much lower rate. If you have the resources to offer a premium (a mouse pad or T-shirt), the return rate will probably increase.

Chapter 8

How to Determine Your First Title or Project

First-time writers are always told, "Pick what you know and write about that." The same can hold true for a multimedia title or project. This does not mean you will be successful selling an interactive kiosk on pig farming in Utah, for example, just because you know all about it. You still have to consider the market for your title. You have to create the right product on the right medium with the right content for the right price.

Look at the Market and See What's Needed

What is the first thing to do? Review the market and find out what is missing. Look at Redgate's *World of Macintosh Multimedia* and the other sources described in Chapter 15. If you and all of your friends have complained that you can't find a really good CD-ROM for your children about butterfly collecting, you may want to create one yourself.

Before you start photographing your butterfly collection, you should take a good look at your own capabilities. Have you studied the subject of your project? You don't necessarily need a degree to produce a multimedia product. However, if you are producing a resource material you should be an expert or at least extremely well-versed in the subject matter. Besides, qualifications help sell the product. If you are not well-known you may want to obtain celebrity endorsement. You don't need a movie star, although that wouldn't hurt. By getting someone your audience would recognize, or even someone from a company or institution your audience would recognize, you will benefit from his or her recognition factor. You must also consider the level of sophistication of the audience.

If most butterfly collectors already know about the life cycle of a butterfly, cover this topic briefly and concentrate on more advanced topics. If few collectors are on the Internet but many have a CD-ROM drive, produce a CD-ROM instead of operating an on-line service.

Localization

When considering your market, don't forget cultural and market localization. If your market is world-wide, avoid local idioms, sayings, and characters. Even if your market speaks the same language as you, and is interested in the same topic, it is not necessarily identical to yours. You have to research your market to know what to avoid. For example, Americans are the only group in the English-speaking world not to use a "u" in words like "colour" and "humour," but few Americans know this.

Your title should describe your topic accurately, and not be excessively broad. If your product reflects a belief that your country, region, or discipline is the center of the world, you will offend people outside your focus who might have bought your product. If the title of your CD-ROM is *Insects* it should be about *all* insects, or at least include a wide cross section of them. If it contains nothing but insects from Australia, for example, buyers will feel misled and will probably be wary of your future products. On the other hand, if the product had been called *Insects of Australia* it probably would have appealed to the same market, who would have enjoyed the particular focus. Understanding your market means selling more products and staying in business after your first project.

In-House Intrigue

In-house corporate developers are approached by other departments to create products for the company. Your mandate is to produce effective products that can be used by a variety of departments. You probably have budget constraints to worry about. Examples of typical in-house projects are multimedia presentations for event support, preparation of interactive sales materials, computer-based training products, and CD-ROM catalogs.

You may think that if you are working in-house you don't have to worry about selling your product or services. In fact, the in-house sales cycle is just as important and possibly more complex than the traditional sales cycle. The process, however, is very different. Everyone working in-house knows that the corporate environment can be extremely political. Many corporate managers want to use multimedia to make them look better. They rely on you to make that happen.

Costing is a significant part of the project. Multimedia projects for a corporation are typically expensive and *you* must justify their costs. Prove to "higher-ups" that your investment will show a return in profit or increased sales or exposure. The problem is that the linkage between profitability and the project itself is not clearly defined and quantifiable. Implementing the project may result in making departments more efficient. The project may increase exposure for a conference or product roll-out. Perhaps it may increase corporate morale. However, it is difficult to quantify these benefits, especially beforehand.

How do you ensure that your group is not seen as an extravagance? Latch yourself to the proper star in the company, and work with him or her to promote each other mutually. You need someone who has the power to protect you from periodic cost-cutting, corporate reorganizations, and changing business trends. You should also be working on internal PR on your own. Make sure that you and your group are not seen as a **cost center**. Write about your group in the company newsletter, taking at least some credit for improvements in the sales, efficiency, or profitability increases. Get testimonial letters from other managers describing how your group's efforts have resulted in some quantifiable improvement for the company. Make sure the important people receive copies of these letters and the newsletter. Be subtle, but not too subtle.

COST CENTER

A department in a corporation with relatively high budget requirements, but without a corresponding return of revenue.

Tips on How to Attract a Producer

The best strategy to get the attention of a producer is to put yourself in the right place at the right time. This means you should go out of your way to speak at trade shows, write for local industry publications, talk at local universities and colleges, appear on talk shows, and do anything to increase your recognition factor. You want to be known as an expert in your particular field and a player in the multimedia industry.

People who assemble trade lists or directories get their names from various sources. First, and perhaps most importantly, they get their names from trade show speaker and attendee lists, newspapers, and magazines. The more a producer sees your name, the more likely you will be called to work on the next big project. Don't overlook charity and not-for-profit groups as valuable sources of contacts. Many people involved with non-profit organizations are also key decision-makers at profitable companies. Exploit these contacts for all they're worth. However, know how to take "no" for an answer. You don't want to alienate your best contacts by coming on too strong. If you do, you won't get another chance to make a pitch for your next project.

An interesting approach is to send a **teaser** to key people in the industry who may hire you or push your product. To promote both yourself and a CD-ROM about canoeing to corporate executives, why not send a paddle to the Vice President in charge of sales? Add a short but provocative note saying, "Don't let your clients go up the creek without this. We can help." Anything more would be overkill. However, always follow up. Sending a brief note or making a call is never considered pushy, but anything more than this can be considered excessive.

TEASER
An advertising gimmick to draw attention to your product or company, often through innovative or outrageous methods.

Finding Your Niche

Multimedia is such a big field that you can't concentrate on more than one or two aspects if you want to be successful. Do you believe, for example, that virtual reality is where the action is? Does your market research support this belief? Have you tailored your in-house expertise, content and talent acquisition, and business plan to support virtual reality production business? Are you prepared to deal with today's limited use of virtual reality? If the answer to each question is "yes," then concentrate on virtual reality products to the exclusion of everything else. This may mean turning away other business like kiosk development. Instead, partner or loosely associate yourself with a kiosk developer whom you respect and trust. That way you can feed off each other's client lists without competing with each other. The key is to stick with what you do best, as long as it pays.

Libraries:
Clip Art, Clip Sounds, Clip Movies

The desktop publishing revolution of the mid-1980s spawned a series of markets for clip art, fonts, and other desktop accessories. The multimedia market is doing the same. Multimedia producers, developers, and publishers are springing up everywhere. In turn, there are great opportunities for those who can provide content for these developers. There is a great demand for interesting, high quality, and diverse clips that can be used in multimedia productions. If you are considering producing a clip library for your first work, remember that every piece of clip art that you include must be cleared through every possible legal channel. However, as long as you are careful about content acquisition, you can produce a low-cost, high-return product with extremely simple software. The following are a few samples of specialization that a developer could choose.

FONTS

Although most uses of fonts are for desktop publishing, they are also used extensively in multimedia projects. Some of the large software developers have produced a wide variety of fonts on CD-ROM format. They can only be accessed by purchasing a password for your particular disc. The fonts are unlocked when you use the password. You may choose to use similar technology to unlock clip art or other elements that can be stored on CD-ROM format. Some purists would suggest that using a CD-ROM merely as a storage device for clip art or fonts is not multimedia, and this – from a purely technical point of view – is true. There is nothing wrong with producing a simple, useful product that sells. Don't think that you have to stuff your multimedia product as full as possible with technological goodies. Always keep your audience in mind. You don't want your audience wondering how you made that effect. You want your audience to concentrate on your message. After all, multimedia is supposed to enhance your learning or entertainment enjoyment. It's not supposed to be a focus unto itself.

APPLICATIONS

Like fonts and clip art, many software applications are being stored on CD-ROM. Since these discs have such a large capacity, they are rapidly becoming an efficient alternative to conventional floppy disks. In a CD-ROM-based software installation, for example, users simply copy over the complete software folder onto their hard drives. Contrast this experience with the shuffling of 10, 20, or even 30 floppy disks to install a complex software package and you'll appreciate why CD-ROMs are being favored as an alternative.

BUSINESS FORMS AND TEMPLATES

With the vast storage capacity available on a CD-ROM there is an incredible opportunity for business and professional products. For example, your products can be a series devoted to a variety of occupations. Create a complete set of standard office documents for every different workplace. Vary the documents if necessary for different jurisdictions. If you can properly customize the product, you can significantly increase your marketing leverage. Be sure to let your lawyer and accountant review this material and add disclaimers to reduce possible lawsuits from people who simply copy your work without modification and get upset when they don't make tons of money.

Electronic documents or templates have been developed for legal offices, financial institutions, and doctors' offices. There is no reason, however, to limit yourself to traditional workplaces. Mechanics need to fill out documentation for each customer and keep careful track of inventory and prices. Semi-professional sports teams have a lot of statistics to keep track of, and templates would make their lives much easier. When you put your mind to it, you'll see that just about any profession, any association, or anyone will benefit from a well-planned template product.

Demos and Tutorials

The low cost of reproducing CD-ROMs makes them the ideal medium for demonstrations or other instructional products. You can create a company that specializes in making demos and tutorials for other companies. Why not contact a number of different software companies and offer – for a small fee – to place their demos on your disc? You can arrange for the disc to be given away free in a relevant magazine, for instance, guaranteeing all participants a large set of prospects. The business advantages to prospects are increased exposure, lead capture, and the use of a better interactive instructional system.

Encrypted Software

There are companies that have bundled many other vendors' software together on one CD-ROM. If computer users see a program they might like, they are able to run a quick demo of the product. If the demo looks good, the package can then be ordered from the CD-ROM by telephoning a toll-free number and purchasing an unlocking code. Manuals can be contained on the disc as well, or they can be shipped to the customer in a few days. Of course, these hardware-specific marketing ideas can only work with computer users who have CD-ROM drives. Considering these devices are rapidly becoming as commonplace as a traditional floppy drive, CD-ROM-based marketing strategies are probably here to stay. Why not piggyback your project with one of these existing CD-ROM-based applications?

The beauty to this method of sales is that distribution costs are minimal and fulfillment time is negligible. The product can be purchased any time and delivered instantly. By bundling your encrypted product with the products of a complementary and mass-distributed product, you will get extensive market penetration for a tiny distribution cost. You will probably have to pay to get into such a deal. You may have to provide one of your best products for free. The bundler wants added value going into its bundle, not mere advertising. Consider how much you can benefit from such a deal, but always keep in mind how much you must pay to get into it.

Chapter 9

Solutions Marketing in the Education World

Students today are much more familiar with technology, computers, and multimedia than are previous generations. Multimedia can be found in their games, their movies, their television programs and, increasingly, in their educational materials. There are approximately 45,000 school boards in the US and 5,000 in Canada, and almost all are using computers in one way or another. Statistics suggest that multimedia helps keep students' interest which, in turn, provides students with more opportunities to learn.

Multimedia in Today's Schools

Multimedia is relatively new to school systems, but it has made a significant impact in a short amount of time. Already, Quality Education Data (QED) – a Denver, Colorado-based research company – reports that 53 percent of the school districts surveyed in 1993 are using multimedia systems in education. Multimedia in schools was virtually nonexistent a scant few years ago. Not every school in these districts uses multimedia systems – in fact, the percentage is relatively low, depending on the demographics – but the numbers are growing rapidly. Obviously, the education market beckons to multimedia companies. However, if you are going to conduct business in the education world, you have to understand that selling into this market is very different from selling to other markets with which you may have experience.

Schools are jumping aboard the multimedia bandwagon because they can now afford to do so. Not only have the prices of related equipment and software declined steadily, but many software vendors and hardware manufacturers offer cut rate pricing to educators and schools. Software discounts, for example, have been known to go as low as 85 percent (or more) to get the education sale.

Why bother to sell at such a discount when the business and consumer channels regularly pay much more? The answer is twofold. Educational discounts are given to encourage teachers and, at the college and university level, professors, to specify particular computer products for the classroom. By almost giving the products away, vendors seek to influence instructors in hopes that they will become indirect sales agents. If an instructor is only or mainly familiar with a particular product, the instructor is more likely to represent it to his or her students as *the* product to use. Students also benefit from educational pricing since this lets them buy a popular product at a great discount. The vendors realize that once these students graduate into the workforce, they will be familiar with and have experience with their products (as opposed to the products of their competitors).

The second reason to offer educational pricing is volume. Selling to educational purchasers often means selling in huge quantities. The decrease in profit from the discount you must offer can be made up for with the high volume of sales. Of course, if you price your products at below cost to get into the educational market, the losses will be multiplied by that same volume. Beware of bankrupting yourself just to get into the educational market. You can only benefit from familiarity with your company name if you are still in business when the students are able to afford your products.

Marketing Multimedia to Schools

Recognizing your own limitations is extremely important, especially for small multimedia companies. Pushing your specialized software or CD-ROM at a few local high schools or colleges is a good idea for any multimedia company. However, if you are a hardware developer or a vendor of general software, you must recognize that you will be competing with the big guys. Microsoft, Apple, IBM, Lotus, and all the other giants are seriously committed to educational markets. They are able to produce their products at a lower cost than most small developers because of the huge volume they produce even without the educational market tie-in. As well, they can afford to offer their products to educational markets at cost – or even less – because they *know* they will be around a few years from now. Many hundreds of millions of dollars are tied up in education institutions purchasing computers, software, and related products. Before you jump on the education bandwagon, you have to understand a few realities.

First, the education sales cycle can be very slow and rocky. Many vendors, for example, don't have the stamina to carry through a year-long recruitment of an education customer. In addition, unlike a business or consumer customer, education customers can be very fickle from one year to the next. Success this year does not necessarily guarantee success the next. This is especially so for boards of education that send out **bid tenders**. It can be very disheartening to be outbid for a huge contract just because of a few dollars per product. Remember, because of the massive purchasing some boards do every year, a couple of dollars (or pounds, deutschemarks, or yen) per product can become magnified into millions over the course of a year.

BID TENDERS
Education facilities often require vendors to submit binding secret offers for prices in quantity for defined products or services.

Second, you should realize that you won't get paid quickly. Some boards are on a regular 90-day payment schedule. This is bad news if your company finances its operations from advance sales. You will have to manufacture and ship the product, support it (if applicable) with high-priced technical people, handle returns, pay your general and administrative expenses like office salaries and rent, all before you can expect to get the board's payment.

Targeting the Decision-Makers

You should also know that education sales can be greatly influenced by politics (both internal and governmental). Frequently, the administrative side of the board might be at odds with the academic side, causing many internal skirmishes you'd be smart to avoid. The administrative side of the board is typically staffed with people who have formal degrees in business, management, or education. Many of these people do not have any direct teaching experience. The administrative group also makes the school's policies. From instructor's pay scales to class size, from the use of professional development days and liaison with the local Parent Teacher Association (PTA), the administration is where it's all decided. Parents have some control over the board through the PTAs or their equivalents, but the boards generally have the final say.

School boards are made up of elected trustees who often have their own agenda, especially if it is an election year. Budgeting may take the upper hand over educational concerns. Trustees must be seen as conforming to board policy even if they disagree with it. Obsolescence is an important issue in the educational market as well. School boards generally have to buy products in large quantities so they must be particularly cognizant of *when* products will need to be replaced. You can convince a school board by showing them your equipment or products will last.

Administrative policies are carried out by the academic staff. Teachers and instructors are often thankful to get any equipment they can. Budgeting constraints in the educational environment are a constant battle for teachers who want to provide their students with the latest information and tools. If you are a small developer, you may find more luck going directly to the teachers or department heads who can use your products. Sometimes, departments have small discretionary budgets that might be tapped for pilot projects. You may wish to lend your products to certain schools, or simply talk to the academic staff to see what they may be able to offer. Don't forget, a good word from several members of the teaching staff will go a long way to influencing the board.

We have been referring to the public school system. The public school system in North America is government-run. In the United Kingdom and other regions, the public school is the equivalent of the North American private school. From a sales viewpoint, there are important differences between the public and private school systems. Generally, private schools are able to spend more money per student and may appear to be a more lucrative market. However, public schools generally have far more students. Private schools like to see themselves as providing better quality education. They recognize the importance of technology to a modern education, but they do not wish to adopt experimental education tools. Most private schools have become computerized, and many schools have CD-ROM drives and some audio/video equipment. There is a huge potential to sell to this market if you go through the proper channels.

It is important to understand the culture in your market. Certain organizations adopt a particular culture, which becomes ingrained and is very hard to change. For instance, if a large corporate organization is built around mainframes you will not be successful selling desktop-based machines. You may encounter pockets of resistance in this culture where desktop multimedia will be used. There are similar differences in platform use because users tend to be brand loyal. The issue for you to determine is that of profitability. Simply put: Is it worth your time to try to change the culture? You will probably not be able to enlighten the entire school board system. You may be able to sell them something, but this won't change the way they do business. Even if they like your products they may choose to purchase from your competitor next year for a variety of reasons. Internal politics, budgeting, or a new policy directive can change your entire business relationship with an educational market in a single day.

How to Get Your Product onto the Approved Vendors List

Every year, vendors are contacted to provide proposals for product sales. One vendor in each category is selected by the school board as the supplier for the entire year. It is not uncommon for one large computer company to be selected as the board's sole supplier. This happens after a long and intensive bid tendering process. Because of their relatively small size, most multimedia developers won't be able to get onto the bid list. However, savvy developers will establish ties to many retailers in the area so that, when the time comes, the computer company that has won the bid will look favorably on the multimedia developer. This in turn means the multimedia developer or production house can establish itself in the role of sub-contractor to the school board. There are usually only one or two vendors for every school in any particular school board jurisdiction.

Find out who the account manager is for the hardware vendor in your area, and negotiate with him or her. You may be able to set up a bundling option for your product with hardware being sold to educational facilities. Perhaps you can include some product literature with every system sold to a particular school system. Every distribution opportunity is a chance for more marketing.

Where to Sell?

QED reports that large school districts with 10,000 or more students are the largest users of multimedia technology. The usage decreases with the enrollment figures. The reasons for this are obvious. The larger school districts have more money and political sway to help them obtain the technology. Besides, the larger school districts are typically in or near the larger cities, where high-tech companies congregate. Fully two-thirds of school districts with large enrollment use multimedia in their instructional curricula, whereas this number decreases to just over one-quarter for school districts with enrollment of under 1,000.

School boards typically invest in technology systems for students in higher grades, figuring that these students will get the most out of the technology. As well, computer and multimedia skills are important in the job market, so the school boards attempt to train their students relatively close to the time when these skills will be in demand. QED reports that 40 percent of its responding districts using multimedia are senior high schools, with the remaining 60 percent split among junior high, elementary, and other school systems.

An important point to note is that, while most schools incorporate computers into their educational programs, few of the computers being used are currently capable of running multimedia software. This is changing. Schools are now recognizing the need to incorporate multimedia into their educational programs. Multimedia in schools generally means the use of CD-ROMs and perhaps a videodisc player. Sound boards and video cameras are lesser used multimedia tools.

Laser discs are still an important market in the educational world, although even this market is slowing. CD-ROM drives are probably the most useful tools of multimedia for education, but their penetration is still relatively low in classrooms. QED's Educational Technology Trends reports in its 1993 – 1994 early estimates that 50 percent of CD-ROM drives in schools are located in libraries with only 25 percent being located in classrooms. However, classroom use of CD-ROM drives is on an increasing trend.

Edutainment

Study after study has shown that people learn more if they are interested in what they are being taught. In addition, people learn a lot more if they are both interested in the subject *and* in control of the learning process. Multimedia allows students to take charge of what they learn, how they learn, when they learn, and what they will do with what they learn. These are key advantages your multimedia project must feature to be successful.

When the barriers to creativity and understanding are taken away, students can learn more and learn better. Students can learn at their own level and pace using multimedia tools. There is no need to wait for the slowest person in the class to catch on; neither is there any need for a student to feel embarrassment if there is a particular point that may take the student longer to understand. Besides, there may be certain points of particular interest on which the students may wish to spend more time. With multimedia, students can explore these subjects without disturbing the rest of the class.

One area of multimedia development that is increasingly gaining popularity is edutainment. Edutainment is a combination of education and entertainment. Companies like Brøderbund, and to a lesser extent Discis, have made their fortunes on edutainment-based CD-ROM content. Its advantage is that children learn without realizing that they are learning.

Discis has pioneered the use of teaching guides that accompany the multimedia versions of their books. By using teaching guides, teachers have lesson plans prepared in advance and they know the points to stress in classroom study. Compare, for example, Edgar Allen Poe's printed poem *The Tell Tale Heart* and the multimedia version of the same poem produced by Discis.

QED expects that fully one-third of all schools in North America will be equipped with CD-ROM drives by next year. This is due to the great job Discis and other multimedia developers have done in providing interesting multimedia content for the educational market. If you intend to sell multimedia to the educational market, the most important thing to do is to put yourself in the shoes of your market. More specifically, consider what teachers can easily incorporate into their lesson plans, and what students can effectively use. Consult with faculty, trustees, and students while developing your project.

Many multimedia firms, such as Discis, are actively recruiting small developers. Why not use the leverage of an established company as a springboard for your sales effort?

Curriculum Development

Multimedia allows teachers to tie together various disciplines and show how subjects relate to each other. For example, many students enjoy baseball, and this can be used to help to teach math. Baseball statistics tell us that major league pitchers often throw fast balls at over 100 miles per hour. If a baseball is traveling at 100 miles per hour, and hits a bat traveling at 50 miles per hour, how can we determine how much energy is generated when the baseball meets the bat? Remember to localize your product to your intended market. Most countries use kilometers instead of miles, so allow your users to select the measurement system in which they wish to work. Multimedia lets you generate an interesting, yet educational, lesson using easily understood concepts.

Increasingly, schools across the United States and Canada have computers available to students and faculty. Audio-visual equipment is equally available. Students are becoming computer literate as a matter of course. Multimedia does not frighten these students any more than television frightened the generations that grew up from the 1950s onward. While there is greater access to multimedia equipment for students in higher grades, even those in lower grade levels become familiar with the general interface and structures used in multimedia. From music videos on television to video-games to movies, multimedia and high-tech communications systems have become part of growing up for today's students.

Trends in K—12 Education

School children are both your most challenging market and your most eager buyers. More than any other age group, the lives of children and adolescents are surrounded by video games, multimedia television, virtual reality, and other types of multimedia on the market. You can't impress today's youth with a few nifty effects. Your aim should be to use multimedia to lead them through the complete educational process. Recognize, however, that parents and teachers are involved in the buying decision, so keep them in mind as you develop your product to appeal to both groups.

Jane Healey, in her book *Endangered Minds*, has hypothesized that television has changed the manner in which a child's brain develops. This means children have been "programmed" differently from the previous non-television generation. Research is continuing in this field and the final results are not expected for some time. From the data already determined, text is no longer the medium of choice for today's youth. Most won't just sit down and read a book. The good news is that they are learning to read in different ways.

In determining what sort of multimedia product to market to educational facilities, you should determine in which particular subjects educators are presently using multimedia. Educators already using multimedia products will likely expand their multimedia base. QED reports that the top areas for multimedia use in teaching are the sciences, social studies, and language instruction. Science classes are most likely to use multimedia at 68 percent, followed closely by social studies at 65 percent, according to QED. At just below 50 percent each, language arts and library and reference are also potential subject markets to target.

SCIENCE, MATH, ENGINEERING

Some school boards have standardized textbooks on CD-ROM or laser disc, with the teacher's edition being different from the students' edition. *Windows on Science* was adopted by the State of Texas for its high school science education program, for example. Students can get a real idea of the subject matter from better visualization. This is especially important in sciences where the subject matter cannot be viewed by the naked eye, such as astronomy and molecular biology. Furthermore, the sciences are subjects in which many students prefer to work at their own pace. Multimedia tools allow students to work at their own speed without sacrificing the benefit of interaction. The only difference is that they are interacting with a computer as opposed to an entire class.

Teachers and school boards will welcome your multimedia educational tools if these tools incorporate everything contained within the board's course outlines. Before you start designing an interactive chemistry CD-ROM, for example, get complete information on next year's curricula. The board will not wish to hide this from you, but don't be surprised if some instructional information is changed drastically at the last minute. The beauty of multimedia, of course, is that these changes can be made relatively quickly and easily if the programming framework is well-designed.

SOCIAL SCIENCES

The main social science to benefit from multimedia is history. History is mainly made up of facts and the storage and quick retrieval of facts are perfect for CD-ROM technology and multimedia display. Teaching with the aid of multimedia can have a far greater impact on students. Pictures, sounds, music, and video images all play upon the emotions, intellect, and psyche. Students can feel like they are experiencing history through an interactive session on the Industrial Revolution, for example. QuickTime movies of the San Francisco earthquake make more of an impact than a listing of statistics ever could. This is the subject area where a multimedia title developer can take greater leeway in putting an educational spin on the product. Because educators are more accustomed to using such entertaining techniques in their educational tools, the title can assume the format and style of a movie or game, rather than that of a lesson.

There is enormous scope in applying multimedia to the social sciences as children do learn more by creating their own fully integrated presentations. The danger is that youthful imaginations can be stifled by having pre-fab creativity at their fingertips. It is important for educators to obtain multimedia products that provide a broad range of ideas. This gives the children the option to form their own opinions and conclusions – in effect, to become independent and successful learners.

LANGUAGES

Those of you who have tried to learn a different language know that you can truly learn the language only by living it. The problem is that you need to repeat words and phrases over and over again before they become second nature. You need someone to correct your grammar and pronunciation. Many people are embarrassed to go through this repetitive process with a person. Multimedia technology allows you inexpensive access to a computerized teacher who is willing to go through constant repetition without complaint or judgment. It also gives you the chance to converse endlessly in a foreign language with "someone" who will always respond in a helpful way. You can make as many mistakes as you like without fear of embarrassment.

Research your target school board's policy before you develop your language product. There is no point developing a Swahili language program if the board has no intention of offering this language in their curriculum.

New Media Centers

The New Media Centers program was founded by a group of high-tech companies with traditional ties to education and interactive media development. Each company has been active in promoting interactive media in higher education. By collaborating, these companies believe they can encourage more schools to benefit from new media more quickly than now possible. These companies have designated the New Media Centers program as the vehicle for corporate support of new media at the university level.

The mission of the New Media Centers program is to form model learning centers for new media technology in institutions of higher education worldwide. These centers serve as resources for training and provide support to a broad range of users: faculty staff, students, instructors, business executives, artists, film makers, and any other interested individuals in institutions of higher education and in the community.

Adobe Systems Incorporated, Apple Computer, Inc., Eastman Kodak, FWB Inc., Macromedia, Prentice Hall, Sony Corporation, and SuperMac are some of the current New Media Center sponsors.

Trends in Higher Education

Many universities and colleges have become incredibly well computerized and networked. Some require laptop computers as a standard educational tool to be purchased by all first-year students. From dorm rooms, students can access many of the "books" in the library. Electronic publishing systems at such universities as Harvard, Cornell, and McMaster print books and course materials on demand. Professors can revise course material a day before the beginning of term and still have them custom-bound and waiting for students for their first class. If these systems are integrated, bookstore obsolescence can be a thing of the past. Copyright approvals are built into the systems and the pricing, so the technology may not be fraught with unnecessary legal fights. These are relatively new systems so all the bugs have not been worked out as yet. Besides, they have not yet been incorporated into all universities.

All of this means that there is a tremendous market in universities and colleges for multimedia tools and content. Processing systems, scanning services, and basic content can all be sold to higher educational institutions. However, large computer companies like Apple, Microsoft, Xerox, and IBM entered the market many years ago. They are well-established and well-heeled. A small or medium-sized software or hardware company may find it difficult to compete head to head with these major software and hardware providers. There is plenty of opportunity for multimedia companies in the service and multimedia content markets. Besides, the more customization you can offer to a school, the more the school administrators will be turned on to your products or services.

Chapter 10
Solutions Marketing in the Business World

The driving force behind the desktop revolution has been business. From the evolution of the large mainframe computer systems contained in specially designed clean rooms to the desktop personal computer, the world of business has shaped and controlled the way we use computer technology. As you might expect, businesses have discovered the value of multimedia and have started implementing its new technology in a variety of ways. Experience has shown that the top uses of multimedia in the business world are for archiving, general communications, collaborative work, presentations, and education and training. Since each one of these general categories uses multimedia in different ways, we will be looking at each opportunity separately.

Archiving

Archiving is concerned with storage and retrieval. CD-ROMs are ideal for this purpose because they can hold large amounts – up to 650 Mb or more – of information efficiently, effectively, for long periods, and with low space requirements. If you plan on using an archiving angle to sell multimedia technology, you can target businesses that need to retain safely many rooms full of information, but which do not require the actual documents. Show your prospects how you can scan all their material onto a CD-ROM and have the information available to anyone in the office in minutes using your special retrieval software.

Examples of businesses that would find this useful are medical facilities, accounting offices, departments of governments, or retail store chains that may want to keep a record of their sales records and staff performances for future reorganizations. Information is key to company reviews, so many companies may find multimedia archiving attractive. The benefit of using a multimedia tool for archiving is its ability to incorporate all aspects of the information being stored. Audio, video, text, graphics, and photographs can be stored on multimedia databases in digital form with perfect reconstitution.

Archiving also relates to data management. Some corporate information must be used on a daily basis while other information is stored only for the sake of evidence. Lists of key people in various parts of your client's industry should be instantly available for retrieval. Your retrieval software should be able to prioritize the information being entered under the guidelines provided by the client. This means that you need excellent communication with your client from the onset to collect this information.

You should also recognize that some professions have not accepted multimedia storage as a viable method of archiving. For reasons of evidence, for example, legal firms must keep original paper copies of documents. Despite the claims of those who tout the paperless office, paper is here to stay. However, the amount of businesses objecting to multimedia storage is growing smaller as the technology becomes more and more a part of everyday life.

General Communications

General communications from a multimedia standpoint entail e-mail and other messaging, networking, and mass communications software technologies. Most offices with more than one or two computers are networked together. The ability to communicate almost instantaneously with the computer of a co-worker and to share files and information is one of the most important changes to the modern office. Computer networking, especially of a plug-and-play variety, is responsible for increases in productivity and widespread participation in the decision-making process.

The integration of electronic mail and multimedia allows workers to bring corporate messages to life. Their inter-office messages can include far more than merely text or words. Still photographs, voice annotations, and full-motion video, to name a few options, can now all be shared in electronic mail. Electronic mail and other similar technologies are implemented from the top level down, usually through the Management Information Services (MIS) or Information Center (IC) groups. To sell to the market, it helps to have experience working in the industry – especially in the MIS or IC groups. From this experience, you can develop contacts with those who will make the purchasing decisions.

Typically, this market is occupied by the large players, including AT&T, Northern Telecom, and Siemens Nixdorf. Small multimedia developers generally cannot compete with these players. What you may be able to do is partner with one of these giants. This can be done either formally through a joint-venture agreement or by providing an additive solution to an existing software. This add-on may make the existing software faster, more effective, or more customized. The bottom line is that you can capitalize on any market no matter how closed it appears at first glance.

Collaborative Work

Following on the heels of communications is collaborative work. Northern Telecom's Visit and Intel's ProShare are video-conferencing and work collaboration products. Both these products represent the growing trend toward interactivity and leveraged usability in the workplace. Video mail, or v-mail, allows for network-wide broadcasting of video messages. Video conferencing allows for point-to-point video interaction.

Many large companies already have the infrastructure in place to implement v-mail. As you might expect, major computer vendors have already jumped on the v-mail bandwagon. Some of these vendors have introduced display monitors sporting built-in cameras as well as video and audio jacks. Industry powerhouse Intel brought out its video conferencing-in-a-box solution and both Radius and Truevision, a division of RasterOps, have released products with which you can capture full-frame, full motion video as well as CD-quality audio.

These systems are relatively expensive at present, but are expected to become less expensive and more powerful over time. In addition to the video hardware and software, these systems need large hard drives of one gigabyte or more and wide network bandwidth if you want to send your information around the company. You might have to set up dedicated video servers to do more than send just a few messages.

Network planning in the v-mail world is significantly different from traditional LAN use. In v-mail-based computing, all message packets have to arrive at the destination exactly when they need to be there. If the video and the audio tracks aren't there (and properly synchronized) when the movie starts playing, the result is jerky frames and playback that skips. Companies in the v-mail market refer to this guaranteed delivery requirement as the "Federal Express" delivery model since your customers won't be happy if the entire message doesn't arrive on time.

The required technology for v-mail and video conferencing is still not readily available in the workplace. Most computers are not equipped with cameras, and some are not even equipped with microphones. Collaborative work technology such as video conferencing and v-mail will take some time to be adopted.

Business Presentations

The use of multimedia in business presentations is one of the most popular, easiest, and most effective uses of the technology today. The Business Research Group (BRG) estimates that 50 percent of the Fortune 1000 companies will be using CD-ROM-based multimedia business presentations by mid-1995. Multimedia business presentations have proven much more effective than thoses based on traditional slides or overheads. Not only is your audience more interested by the drama and humor available with multimedia, but the presentations themselves are more effective.

Speakers can modify their presentations, depending on the interests of the audience. Changing information can be modified as the presentation is going on for a truly up-to-the-minute effect. Multimedia presentations generally have high production values while keeping costs per presentation low because they can allow for repurposing of effects and transitions. Most importantly, multimedia business presentations allow for interaction to a much greater extent than do traditional business presentations. As we discussed in Chapter 9, interaction allows for better education. People learn more when they are involved in – and in control of – the learning process. Similarly, business people learn more when they are involved in the business presentations designed to teach and inform them.

Many companies are hiring out top business presentation consultants both to prepare the presentations and to give the presentations. Hired guns are rarely used to set up deals with potential partners or clients because these clients generally want to see that the business people themselves know what they are talking about. However, business presentation consultants are often called in for annual general meetings, trade shows, and internal corporate events. These consultants combine humor with a quality look and feel to entertain the audience with the information or corporate vision being presented. Their function is to increase corporate morale while they inform and inspire.

To grab your piece of the multimedia business presentations market, start by building a small but loyal clientele. Attend local shows or small events where you can learn the ropes, and work in conjunction with a known audio-visual company. A background in public speaking, music, or even college drama can be a great help in this business. Learn to modularize your presentations. This means that you can repurpose some parts of your presentation so as not to duplicate your efforts. A client need not know that you reuse some presentation elements from time to time. Besides, since you will customize it to the particular company, they shouldn't care.

Trade show kiosks are being used by more and more companies who want to increase their exposure. These kiosks can be stand-alone or accompanied by a presenter, but they always include multimedia. If a company is part of an industry with a large number of trade shows, sending kiosks to these shows instead of or in addition to staff can be extremely cost-effective. Kiosks never get tired and can be placed anywhere. Even now, many companies outside the technological industries are starting to use kiosks as an integral part of their trade show presentation gear. However, there is a large potential market that does not yet realize the value a corporate kiosk could be to their business. It's up to you to tell them.

Another growing side business for business presentations companies is the creation of multimedia product catalogs. Increasingly, businesses are adopting these product catalogs as an indirect sales force. Some companies have created collaborative interactive CD-ROM catalogs, incorporating the products of various companies in a wide variety of categories. The *En Passant* project successfully sold almost US$40,000 worth of apparel, electronics, children's items, office supplies, and other items in a two-month test period. The companies that tend to offer their own multimedia catalogs are multimedia-related companies like Afga, Adobe, or clip art companies.

Corporate Education and Training

Multimedia education in businesses means training, retraining, education on corporate policies and procedures, safety training, and just-in-time training. Multimedia can make all of these more effective. Computer-based training (CBT) can be done when the worker has time, or when the worker most needs the education. Furthermore, the worker can learn at his or her own pace, and concentrate on the issues of particular interest. BRG estimates that 30 percent of Fortune 1000 companies are already using CD-ROM-based multimedia training, and the number is growing rapidly.

Training is sometimes combined with business presentations to create team-based skills training. These sessions may take place at conventions or corporate retreats. They are designed to teach new ways of thinking.

As businesses and home offices increasingly get wired for the information superhighway, video on demand (VOD) will become more and more important. Presently, VOD allows corporate workers to get information about company's events, job postings, and even the latest quote for the company's stock by simply accessing a station on the network or stand-alone kiosk located within the workplace. Furthermore, it allows for improved product demonstrations. Industry experts expect the use of VOD to increase.

Understanding the Players in a Large Corporation

If you are part of a large corporation or if your customers or prospects are large corporations, you would be well advised to find out all you can about the players involved. Your first step is to get an organizational chart of the company. This should list who heads up what divisions, who works on what projects, and who doesn't. Past organizational charts will also assist you in determining who's on the fast track and whose career is stalled. Find out who the decision-makers are, who the influencers are, and who the users are. Find out who (really) calls the shots.

The way to find out these critical points is to analyze the company culture. In some companies organizational charts are confidential. This is done primarily to prevent an executive recruiter or headhunter from luring managers to other firms. In addition, some companies – such as large American or British conglomerates – feel that releasing organizational charts to outsiders poses a security risk and places their employees in potentially unsafe situations. Word to the wise: Be sensitive to your target company's feelings in this matter. Be creative in learning all you can about your market. An employee sympathetic to your mission may help you draw your own organizational chart over a long lunch.

Look at the company culture and internal workings. How do people dress? Suit and tie or casual? Is work done collaboratively or autonomously? To fit into a corporation you have to act like one of them. To market to a corporation you have to be able to create a product that will fit into their corporate culture.

It's a safe bet that most senior executives won't have a lot of time for you. If you suspect this is the situation at your target company, work from within. Assistant to the president, VPs, office managers, and even (often especially) secretaries are important since they control access to the boss (whoever he or she is). If you understand who the players are you'll be able to navigate more effectively through the office politics.

Foremost to any sales pitch – regardless of the size or type of target company with which you are dealing – is answering one simple question: "What can I do to help you?" This is the question you must always keep uppermost in your mind through your sales pitch, through product development, through delivery and support. If you can successfully convince your prospects that you will help them in their jobs then you will get the multimedia sale. How can buying your product – or service – create more money, raise the prestige, or increase the visibility of your prospect? Can your product or service bolster his or her career? Of course it can. When you help make managers look good to peers and bosses, they will want to use you and your company again and again.

Remember that selling to the business world is extremely political. If a manager makes the wrong decision he or she may lose his or her job. Cultivate as many sponsors as possible in a given company.

Review the information in Chapter 5 before planning a sales call.

Understanding the Sales Cycle in a Large Corporation

Some salespeople think that getting a sales presentation is the final step in the corporate sales cycle when, it, fact, it is just one of the first steps. Purchasing generally starts at the committee stage. Potential needs are determined by the various committees who make up a list of requests for purchase, often in order of priority. These requests are taken to a purchasing meeting by the committee head. Once the potential purchase has been approved and budgeted, sales presentations are requested by the major competitors in the industry. Many large orders in a corporation are put out to bid. This will ensure that the company gets the best price, and that no improprieties take place in the order process.

In some companies, the purchasing department makes all the sales overtures. In others, an individual manager controls his or her department's budget. Typically, managers in large corporations have a departmental budget that is agreed to once a year. They are penalized if they spend more than their budget. The best time to give a sales pitch for a small project is just after the budgets have been approved and the departments are flush with cash. For larger projects, long-term sales strategies may be needed. Find out when the company's fiscal year begins to cash in on the best periods. Budgets may be determined annually, semi-annually, or quarterly. Usually there is a formal budget planning time of between three and six months prior to the beginning of the actual period. Get an annual report for the company and call up administrative agents within the company. They will generally tell you anything you want to know. If it is a public company, buying a few shares means that you will be sent important shareholder information periodically.

Working with a Non-Technical Business or Entrepreneur

Many small business people see the awesome sales potential of multimedia and want to jump on the bandwagon. Unfortunately, many of these business people have no idea of what multimedia is or what it can add to their particular business. You want these people as clients, but you must treat them delicately. Many believe the hype that technology can allow you access to infinite amounts of targeted information instantaneously, and they believe that multimedia software can be customized quickly, easily, and inexpensively.

These people need to be educated. Multimedia and technology in general may not be able to perform the magic that they expect, but you will probably be able to impress them with the opportunities available. Show them case studies of how their competition has improved their bottom line through use of multimedia. There is a wide variety of articles detailing the use of multimedia and general technology in the workplace. Save these and use them to your benefit, even if they are not about your company. Go through the basic possibilities of e-mail, just-in-time training, and business presentations before trying to sell them on applications that are too high-tech. Otherwise, you will scare off a likely prospect.

Check out Multimedia Demystified — A Guide to the World of Multimedia from Apple Computer, Inc. listed in Chapter 15 for good case studies.

What Businesses Look for in a Multimedia Vendor

As we mentioned earlier, customers want a trustworthy partner with whom to conduct business. Your customers are primarily concerned with whether you can do the job and won't go out of business. References and demonstrations help to calm their concerns. Keep in mind that the person who signs the purchase order at the company is sticking out his or her neck for you. You must assure your customer that everything will go according to plan, within budget, and on time.

Customers – big or small – hate surprises.

What Types of Businesses Are the Best Targets for Your Projects

Starting salespeople are taught that to clinch a sale, your prospect has to be three things: ready, willing, and able to make a purchase. To ensure success in the multimedia sale process, there are a few things to watch for. Scout out managers who understand and want technology. They will go bat for you internally.

Scan the pages of local or regional magazines and newspapers for articles on companies adopting new technology. Then look for their competitors. A company whose competitors have already gone high-tech will likely be more responsive to the suggestion that they need to catch up.

Look for companies that can specifically benefit from one or more of the five general categories described at the beginning of this chapter. Communication is especially important to companies with many departments that have to collaborate on projects. Companies that frequently need to communicate to a large number of people in disparate departments may be getting more and more frustrated with the traditional systems they have. Companies that have recently expanded or merged are always good prospects for your sales pitch. The new workers or the newly merged sides wish to demonstrate their grasp of the future of the company. How better to do this than to promote technological advancement for the company? Companies that are going through a reorganization may also be good prospects, but they must be approached carefully. It is difficult to know which players will survive a reorganization, or who will be in power in the end. You want to avoid alienating those who may be the top influencers tomorrow, so make blanket approaches to these companies.

What Projects Have the Best Chance of Success

Multimedia business presentations are very popular at present. They are wide-ranging and can be used in almost any industry. Don't go into this field without the proper entertainment background or support. What you are looking for is long staying power. Ideally, you want to develop a long-lasting relationship with a company for the production of all of their business presentations, related trade show kiosks, and other business products.

Communications systems are being implemented in all the major companies and government offices. However, the systems being implemented are those of the industry giants. Networking powerhouses like Novell, Intel, and Microsoft, along with the hardware giants, currently have the business communications markets sewn up. You can get involved by providing add-on services to these communications systems, or by working with one of the giants to create an additional service. Do not try to compete head on with the giants in this area.

Training manuals are a great area for market prospecting. The digital revolution has affected more than just technology industries, and many companies find they must retrain staff more often. The newest technologies often succeed in the business environment because of the support that large numbers of staff can give. For example, CD-Recordable (CD-R) is being advanced through businesses more than anywhere else. This technology is most useful in businesses where multiple uses of content make the highly priced CD-R equipment more cost-effective. The price of this equipment is falling drastically as is the price of a blank CD-R disc, which has declined from US$150 per disc to just over US$10.

In the end, the most successful multimedia projects are the ones that complement a company without being intrusively technical. The multimedia aspects of a business solution should make the project more effective, more efficient, and more fun. The goals of a multimedia solution are the same for any business project – to increase the bottom line. Multimedia solutions do this by making people work better, by saving storage space, by increasing morale, and by putting a better face on a business.

Chapter 11

Solutions Marketing in the Consumer and Home Markets

The Potential Market for Consumer Titles and Content

The consumer market for CD-ROM titles has grown considerably in recent years due to the decrease in price of CD-ROM drives – currently selling at US$200 and up – and to the large number of consumer CD-ROM titles on the market. The adoption of CD-ROM technology as the predominant delivery medium has been pivotal to the success of multimedia in the home and consumer markets. Many consumers think only of CD-ROM technology when they think of multimedia. Inteco Corporation – a Norwalk, Connecticut-based multimedia research company – forecasts that 1995 computer-based CD-ROM drive sales will be roughly 10 million units. In Europe, CD-ROM drive sales are forecast to be about 2.5 million units with sales in Japan estimated to be 1 million units. By 1997, Inteco forecasts that the home market installed-base will total 40 million in the USA, over 11 million in Europe, and almost 5 million in Japan.

The same study indicates that by 1997 up to 45 percent of all households in North America will have CD-ROM drives. In 1993, sales of CD-ROM drives to the home market grew more than all other markets, accounting for 62 percent of all the drives shipped, equating to almost 4 million drives. Inteco also found that the number of CD-ROM titles designed for home use (that is, games and entertainment) roughly doubles every year. At this rate, Inteco forecasts that by 1997, 75 percent of the 40 million installed CD-ROM drives will be found within the home.

Prices for both drives and titles are dropping rapidly, reducing the investment risk for purchasers. The technology continues to improve with faster seek and transfer rates, increased capacity and longevity of storage media, and easier to understand software and interfaces. Home computer users are beginning to use multimedia titles to assist them in everyday tasks. From cookbooks to budgets to golf instruction to reference materials, multimedia titles have made a great impact on the consumer marketplace. This means that there is great scope to develop and sell your products and services, but you must recognize the impressive competition that has already entered the marketplace.

How to Sell to the Consumer Market

Review Chapters 4 and 5 for the basics on multimedia marketing and sales. There are some important issues to consider when selling to the consumer market that are different from selling to educational or business markets. First of all you must recognize that there is considerable competition and the price of entry is high, especially in established markets like those for encyclopedias. (However, the latest technology allows developers to enter the market with a *relatively* smaller investment than in previous years.) More significantly, entertainment giants such as Paramount and Disney have made considerable investments in the future of multimedia, through research and development, content acquisition and licensing, advertising, and through the purchase or creation of independent companies.

This does not mean that the market is over-saturated or that there is no room for you. **Distributors** are always looking for great content. **Retailers** and mail order houses are always on the lookout for the next best-seller. Great content is marketable content. It may be intellectually stimulating. It may be well researched and complete. Or it may be simply entertaining. For a title to be successful, it must have a good chance of selling in large quantities

DISTRIBUTORS
Organizations that purchase products from hardware manufacturers and software developers and resell these products to retailers or direct to consumers.

RETAILERS
Organizations that sell products to customers, usually from a store-front operation.

at high margins. Certain distributors specialize in consumer markets, and may have very narrow specializations within the consumer market. You can determine which distributors might be for you by considering what titles they specialize in and the demographics toward which they market.

Meet the Giants of Consumer Publishing and Distribution

If you are looking for a publishing or distribution venture with one of the industry giants or major distribution houses, you had better know whom to approach. In the consumer market, you generally need to sell large quantities of your product to be profitable. Some of the multimedia giants have special programs for beginner developers. In this chapter, we provide some of the companies active in the multimedia industry from a development, publishing, or distribution viewpoint. Due to competitive pressure, most companies decline to discuss royalty fees and license arrangements with their (potential) business partners over the telephone. Contact more than one company and shop the market as best you can.

We have included a contact procedure for each company where applicable and possible. Contact information is listed in Chapter 15.

Brøderbund Software, Inc. –
DEVELOPER, PUBLISHER, AND DISTRIBUTOR

DEVELOPER
An organization that brings multimedia products from the idea stage to the finished product stage.

PUBLISHER
An organization whose principal role is to bring to market multimedia products.

Brøderbund, one of the giants in the multimedia distribution industry, publishes many CD-ROM titles in North America and internationally. Its better known titles include *Where in the World Is Carmen Sandiego?* and *MacGlobe*. Examples of its multimedia titles include *Arthur's Teacher Trouble* and *Just Grandma and Me*. Brøderbund concentrates on publishing edutainment and children's educational titles, and has an affiliate label program and a third-party publishing program.

Claris Clear Choice –
Developer, Publisher, and Distributor

Claris is a subsidiary of Apple Computer, Inc. The company's Clear Choice program finds, evaluates, and publishes software developers' titles in the multimedia entertainment and educational markets. Claris encourages developers to submit existing titles for evaluation and possible publication.

Compton's New Media –
Developer, Publisher, and Distributor

Compton's, one of the most important players in the multimedia market, has an extensively diverse range of titles in cross-platform formats. Its *Interactive Encyclopedia* is perhaps its best-known and most successful title. However, it also distributes games, entertainment, and educational titles. Other popular titles include *Science & Nature*, *The King James Bible*, *USA Today*, and *The Complete Beatles*. The company has a very active third-party developer program. It will repackage your product to fit physically within its retail in-store racking and allow you to sell your products with its products. Compton's currently represents over 50 third-party titles, many on different hardware platforms, and has more than 100 titles in total in its distribution lists, including those from third-party programs and those developed in-house.

Corel Systems –
Developer, Publisher, and Distributor

Corel actively seeks out third-party photographic content that it then packages into a retail-ready product – Corel's CD-ROM XA Kodak PhotoCD disc series. According to the company, Corel currently has a stable of hundreds of titles and adds new ones every month. If you are an amateur photographer you might be interested in Corel's program. One thing you should know, however, is that publishing your photography with Corel is not very lucrative relative to typical professional photography fees, and developers are usually required to give up all licensing rights to their work. However, this may be a good introduction to CD-ROM development and many first-time developers have made deals with Corel. There is much controversy among professional photographic organizations over the impact series of this nature have on the value of an image and the profitability of photography.

Discis Knowledge Research, Inc. –
DEVELOPER, PUBLISHER, AND DISTRIBUTOR

Discis develops, publishes, and distributes cross-platform titles internationally, being best known for its children's books on CD-ROM. Its most notable titles include *The Night Before Christmas* and *The Tale of Peter Rabbit*. As well, it has an on-going joint marketing deal with the National Geographic Society (NGS) in which Discis provides programming expertise, a proprietary search and retrieval engine, and the basic look and feel of a Discis product. From this, NGS is able to develop multimedia titles by adapting its content for the Discis format. Discis is actively recruiting developers for single stand-alone discs as well as complete series.

Disney Software –
DEVELOPER AND PUBLISHER

Disney Software is a subsidiary of The Walt Disney Company. Because of its relationship to one of the legendary content providers, Disney Software is able to publish highly recognizable titles, including games and products relating to *Beauty and the Beast* and *Aladdin*. It publishes CD-ROMs and floppy software in cross-platform formats.

Educorp –
DEVELOPER, PUBLISHER, AND DISTRIBUTOR

Educorp concentrates on educational and informational multimedia products. Its titles are distributed through mail order on CD-ROM and floppy discs on both Macintosh and PC platforms. Educorp's top titles include versions of desktop publishing, clip art, and Educorp Shareware. The company actively recruits developers. The first step for a new developer is to telephone the company and ask for a product submission kit. Return the completed paperwork and include a working copy of your title complete with packaging. Educorp's technical support group will evaluate your submission and advise its marketing counterpart of your product's likelihood of success. Through a relatively simple formula – explained in the kit – Educorp may then offer space in its catalog in exchange for representation of your CD-ROM product. Educorp is arguably the most important catalog for CD-ROM developers in North America, due to its impressive market penetration. The company has a strong presence in the home/consumer market as well as the education market as a result of its many shareware CD-ROMs. You can also license video clips through Educorp.

Euro-CD –
DISTRIBUTOR

Euro-CD is a CD-ROM distribution company that represents many North American titles in Europe. It carries out marketing, sales, and distribution of products in conjunction with its catalog and order mechanism. If you have an existing title that is selling well in the North American market, consider approaching Europe through Euro-CD. Analyze the potential market forces and localization factors before you approach Euro-CD. Titles on baseball or North American-specific television shows, for instance, may not sell in large numbers in Europe, whereas adventure games are universally successful as long as language translation and other cultural issues are not problematic. Euro-CD actively seeks CD-ROM titles with a proven track record. In your submission, include a cover letter, a product sample, a brief sales history of units sold, units, and retail price.

Grolier Electronic Publishing, Inc. –
DEVELOPER AND PUBLISHER

Like Compton's New Media, Grolier is another developer and publisher best-known for its encyclopedia. It also distributes the *Guinness Multimedia Disc of Records*. Grolier distributes titles on CD-ROM and floppy disk in cross-platform formats, but concentrates on educational compilation titles.

Philips Interactive Media of America –
DEVELOPER, PUBLISHER, AND DISTRIBUTOR

Philips is a subsidiary of its Holland-based parent. It has wide-ranging deals with such content providers as Paramount Pictures, ABC, Hanna Barbera, Time Warner Interactive, Polygram, Nintendo and, of course, Philips Electronics. Philips created the CD-ROM with Sony Corporation, so the vast majority of its titles are on its proprietary format, CD-Interactive (or CD-I), which uses television as its customary output device. The diverse subjects of the titles range from sports to music to children's entertainment.

Time Warner Interactive –
DEVELOPER AND PUBLISHER

Time Warner Interactive (TWI) distributes through retail outlets, and has the popular titles and marketing clout to dominate store shelves. This content giant repackages its own material on CD-ROM, CD-I, Laserdisc and Macintosh floppy. It has also created games as well as interesting historical perspectives such as its retrospective on Desert Storm and its profile on Bill Clinton. This company also distributes such informational and entertaining titles as *Woodstock, How Computers Work,* and *The View from Earth.*

The Voyager Company –
Developer, Publisher, and Distributor

Voyager distributes cross-platform CD-ROMs for the entertainment, educational, and general consumer markets through a catalog for international sales. Top titles include *A Hard Day's Night* and *Baseball's Greatest Hits*. There is a Voyager Expanded Book Toolkit that allows you to create your own electronic books with the same simple features found in many of Voyager's titles. The Expanded Book Toolkit is available for less than US$300 and is likely the least expensive way of taking existing content and adding a multimedia touch. Once in expanded book format your content can be marketed by Voyager in its catalog. Royalty and licensing fees vary from project to project.

Wayzata Technology, Inc. –
Developer and Publisher

Wayzata distributes a wide variety of CD-ROM titles, including *Ocean in Motion*, *Space Time*, and *Art and Supertoons*. Based in Grand Rapids, Michigan, the company's targeted markets include educational, entertainment, and general consumer sectors.

Focusing on CD-ROM Title Subjects

To be successful, small and medium-sized developers must be able to focus on a particular area. More important, you need a clear vision to focus your marketing efforts. It's very easy for small titles and companies to get lost in the marketing hype of the industry. This is especially true in the consumer sector since it typically takes a lot of money to get your message out to the purchasing public. The Coca-Cola Company and PepsiCo spend millions of dollars annually advertising soft drinks. Obviously an interactive game, business presentation software, and other multimedia products require more explaining than does a cola. Choose your market wisely to stretch your advertising and marketing budget.

Reference

Compton's, Microsoft, and Grolier have already released general multimedia encyclopedias each incorporating thousands of articles and still photographs, and many minutes of full motion video, graphics, and audio. These giants have also produced general dictionaries and thesauruses, or they represent the companies that have produced them. A large amount of time, money, labor, and legal work is required for a complete work of this sort. Because of this, only a major developer has the bandwidth to produce titles to compete with such exhaustive products. One must invest hours developing content that must be researched, summarized, verified, entered, and rewritten. However, you can still position yourself in the reference market by focusing on specific subjects. Anything that can be cataloged can be referenced and brought to life in a multimedia product. CD-ROMs are ideal for reference products because of their storage capacity. Subjects such as animals, stamps, cars, diseases, movies, or computer systems can be made into reference CD-ROM titles.

Games

Games are divided into two broad categories: strategy and action. CD-ROM discs are excellent media for strategy games because of the vast capacity of storage and resultant opportunity to increase game complexity. A strategy/adventure game can incorporate hundreds of different branches in the program, resulting in hundreds of different scenarios. When you incorporate multimedia into games you bring the entire experience to life, adding more realism and believability. Adventure games are particularly dependent on the impact of the entertainment side of multimedia to keep the game interesting. Even so, the adventure games that sell best require significant reasoning power on the part of the player.

Production of these games requires many **person-months** for planning, programming, and testing. Experienced game designers may take a year or more to produce a single game. These types of strategy or adventure games may be too expensive for a beginning multimedia company to bring to market unless it is well-funded. If you have significant experience in this field, or can link up with existing game producers, you can develop titles within six to eight months. It should be stressed that these are estimates only. Your results will depend on your team's programming expertise, the complexity of your game, whether or not you develop a cross-platform game, and many other factors. If you're like most developers, development costs will shrink drastically from the first to the second title because most of your R&D and programming code can be repurposed.

> **PERSON-MONTHS**
> The politically correct term for the amount of work that can be reasonably completed by a worker in an average month. This is an average number being determined by adding the output of all of the workers on a given project and dividing it by the number of months required to complete the work.

Maps/Directories

Creating multimedia cartographic products is an interesting but risky business. This is especially so in these changing political times when domestic and international boundaries are redrawn from week to week. The best tactic here is to form a strategic partnership with the companies who own the content. Once you have developed the tools to search and display maps, it is conceptually a simple task to enter the appropriate data into your program to have a new title. The difficulty is to avoid dating your product as much as possible. Once you have developed your **search engine** you can update the information in your product from time to time, when appropriate.

> **SEARCH ENGINE**
> Programming code that allows quick search and retrieval for multimedia content.

Sports/Leisure

Many multimedia sports titles have been released into the market driven by the overwhelming interest in sports. There is great scope to sell to the sports market because opinions on sports vary and different people enjoy sports in different ways. The challenge is to entice consumers who enjoy a particular sport into experiencing a computerized multimedia version of that sport. Creating an interactive experience works when you include instructional material, humor, and a wide variety of options.

The major markets for sports titles varies by geographic region. The major North American contact sports are football, basketball, and hockey. The non-contact sports are baseball, golf, skiing, and racquet sports such as tennis. Golf is also the major sport in Japan, along with sumo wrestling. In Europe the major sport is soccer. This analysis also applies to leisure activities and hobbies that can be transformed into CD-ROM titles.

Interactive Literature

Voyager's *Expanded Books* are excellent examples of interactive literature. Any story that can incorporate interesting visual aspects, music, or sound effects can benefit from multimedia. Interactive literature has been promoted most effectively through the success of children's books on CD-ROM. Within a few years, there will be a reading audience who has learned to read, at least partially, through interactive literature. The market will expand as the installed base of CD-ROM drives continues to increase. As the public becomes more accustomed to the concept of an interactive book we will see an increasing demand for all sorts of titles and a broader scope to the titles being developed.

The Voyager Company is an example of a successful company that has concentrated its efforts on interactive multimedia books for adult markets. It is recognized as one of the leaders in the burgeoning multimedia industry. Get creative in your R&D, but look to the leaders in the interactive literature field for a basic framework within which to work. Interactive books promise to be a stepping stone from which even more interesting innovations are likely to grow.

Chapter 12

Press Relations — why YOU need it!

Most technical people don't know what PR means. If this sounds like you – or someone you know – this chapter can help. Press relations can create the best advertising you can possibly get. A good editorial or review of your product is far more credible than any paid advertising ever could be. Most public relations experts estimate that editorials have, on average, between three and seven times the weight of advertising. Added to this is the comparatively low cost of press relations. An ad in a city newspaper can cost thousands, while a review costs nothing – at least in cash. Press relations do cost you time and effort. However, it is invariably worthwhile. You may also consider hiring a professional PR firm or press agent to help your product get coverage. All of these issues will be discussed in this chapter.

Meet the Players

Press is the collective reference word for people working on stories for newspapers, magazines, books, and newsletters. Radio and television reporters are usually referred to as "the media."

There are important differences between the press and the media. If you are approaching them your approaches should be different. Put simply, the press is looking for something that looks good on paper, while the media is looking for something that will look and/or sound good on a radio or television broadcast. The press wants a short, catchy headline that is easy to read and says the entire story. The media wants a phrase that grabs your attention and makes you want to stay tuned.

The most the press can use along with a story is still photographs. The press speaks through the words it chooses to print. The media can interview you live on camera, capturing all the action, color, and style of your product. It can also show what is lacking, so you have to be well-prepared from a visual standpoint for an interview by the media. No matter what, neither the press nor the media will give you a second chance. And remember, there's no such thing as speaking off the record to a professional reporter or journalist.

While the people within publications or shows generally work together to get the best stories, there is a hierarchy in their ranks. At the top of the heap are the publisher and the editor. The editor typically heads up the creative side of the publication. The editor implements the editorial spin to the publication that the publisher decrees. Assistant editors and associate editors typically head up departments. In a newspaper, for example, the business organization might be headed up by an assistant editor. Reporting to the assistant editor might be a series of staff reporters handling specific departments. The national economy, the local economy, science, popular music, and so on might have staff reporters responsible for covering the news in their specialties.

Freelancers are journalists who sell articles to different newspapers and press agencies. Where a staff reporter works for a particular press outlet, a freelancer sells stories to any publisher who will buy. Freelancers typically spend half of their time trying to sell the story to a publisher, so they have even less time for you. Depending on the type of television and radio program, the people who hold the same status as that of a newspaper editor and publisher are the managing director and the executive producer, respectively.

Approaching the media means approaching the entertainment desks of local and regional news shows, and approaching the research staff for specialized media magazine television shows, such as Toronto-based Media Television.

Many people forget radio in their attempts to get press reviews. Certain stations can be very important to your product sales, specifically university and college stations. They have a large captive audience of the target age group for multimedia use and sales. Increased awareness of your products and company by a college radio station can have the added benefit of increasing your chances of being accepted for sales by the college purchasing agents.

Understanding Press Relations

The press is not out to get you. Frankly, reporters, journalists, and publishers don't care about you one way or the other. The press is out to get stories. If you can provide a good story, the press will listen and print it. If you don't have a good story, the press won't have time to talk to you.

Time is a big issue to the press. Most reporters and writers you will talk to are on a deadline. They have to investigate a story, interview people for it, get all the technical details straight, simplify them, write the story, revise it if necessary, file the story, and then wait for it to get chopped by the editor into something completely unrecognizable. Whether a writer works on a monthly, weekly, or daily publication, a shortness of time remains constant.

Always inform the press of anything new in your company, but make sure that it at least resembles a story. Send off a press release for a new title release, an award, an award nomination, a new technology you have developed, or any other interesting tidbit. If the announcement is big enough call a press conference. Press conferences are staged and stilted, but they are part of life for the press.

Wire services are available to anyone who wishes to post a message and pay the postage. The Associated Press, Reuters, and the Canadian Press all have wire services available at about US$0.25 per word. Every newspaper has access to these services and can pick up any message that interests a reporter. There is no guarantee that listing with a wire service will result in your story getting picked up, but it certainly helps your chances.

Networking with the press is very important. Try to position yourself as a multimedia expert or guru. The press wants people it can call upon for a quick quote on specific subjects. You want the press to think of you. If your company makes games on CD-ROM, the press should know to call you for a comment when new laws come out requiring warning labels for CD-ROM content. Allow yourself to be used as a resource. Be available when reporters need you. Call up people in the press if you think of a good idea for a story, even if it has nothing to do with your company. They will appreciate your help, and they may reward you in the future with extra space in their columns. The press is a tight clique. Concerted effort with a few press contacts could result in important publicity rewards with other members of the press.

Before you can send off your first press release, you have to know whom to inform. The function of press relations should be part of the marketing side of life.

Keep lists of press contacts that write about your types of product or service. If, for example, you make a CD-ROM title, you might scan trade magazines for articles on CD-ROMs. Write or call these people to verify if they cover CD-ROMs. By supplying general newspapers, magazines, or even radio and television with news and information, you help them do their jobs. You can't, however, send them junk and expect any action from them. Press people receive plenty of news releases and telephone calls every day. The job of press relations personnel is to make your press releases stand out.

PRESS RELATIONS

Why You Need It!

Press Kits with One-Offs

If you are a CD-ROM producer, the best way to sell your product is to give it away. You can't get a good review unless the writer knows about your product. This means that you should be sending out samples of your finished product to the press. Microsoft, Claris, Lotus, and many other large computer companies give away skids of software every year to key reporters. Hardware developers set up loaner programs for the press to introduce their technology. However, do not blanket the press with your product. Target members of the press who are likely to print your story, or who might, at least, be interested in your product. Once you have qualified your press list, blanket this targeted press.

When we refer to the targeted press, we are speaking in general terms. Do not wait for a multimedia reporter to be appointed at your local newspaper before you send out a press release. Try sections such as science, business, life style, features, entertainment, or anything related to the content of your product. Major newspapers and specialty publications have at least one reporter or journalist who concentrates on technical matters. It is rare to find a multimedia editor unless you are looking at publications devoted to the computer industry. Multimedia, as its own subject department, has not yet established its place in mainstream journalism.

Your mailing to the press is a sales job, so send out more than just your product. Your press kit should include the following:

Check out a sample press release in Chapter 14.

- a 1- to 2-page news release
- a sample of your software product on diskette, one-off CD-ROM or any other applicable sample format
- background information on your company
- background information on the important or well-known members of your company
- a 4 x 5 black and white photo of your product (for newspapers)
- a 4 x 5 color photo of your product (for magazines)

Increasingly, press relations specialists are sending an electronic version of all of the above along with the paper versions. Electronic press releases can be a terrific help to your company. However, don't get so caught up with the technology that you forget about your audience. A reporter or press writer wants to take a brief look at your material in paper form to assess whether or not you are worth his or her time.

Catch the attention of the reporter and then take him or her down the road you want to travel. A good press release can be made into an entire article with only minor modifications. Press releases should be written in short, very quotable sentences. Explain what the product does, and how it is a solution to a particular problem, want, or need. Explain who should be interested in your product, and why. If your product can possibly have an impact on society, talk about it. Jump on any fashionable bandwagon you can find, but make sure you are up to date.

Even if you don't have a finished CD-ROM-based product, you can still make something impressive to send to the press. One-off machines have become much less expensive in recent years, both to buy and to use at a service bureau. Press releases on a diskette are great, because the writer can use your quotes as you have written them. The more you can simplify a reporter's or reviewer's job, the better the results. If you write your press releases well, you will probably find your own words in the resulting article. Most writers don't have the time to labor excessively over composition. If you provide them with a few good lines, they will probably use them. This does not mean that reporters will believe and print everything you include in a press release. They will probably not use your superlatives to promote you. However, they probably will use your technical descriptions if you have written them in language their readers can understand.

Customizing Your Marketing Material for the Press

Just as you have to design your product to appeal to your market, you have to design your press releases for your press audience. Similarly, if you have a cross-platform product, you have to approach a cross-platform press. Research organizations like Dataquest have found that most multimedia development is done on the Macintosh. However, many press organizations use IBM compatibles to write their articles prior to typesetting for print. Your marketing and press materials, demos, and samples should be prepared on both platforms. This includes references to specific operating systems and other technologies.

Most press people take about 10 seconds to decide whether or not to look into your press kit in detail. This means that if you use terminology that does not suit their platform, they are liable to throw your press kit in the garbage without even looking at your product. If you wait for the second page to say that your product is cross-platform, easy-to-use, designed for the over 50s crowd, or about jazz music, you will probably lose your chance with the press. That means you will inadvertently throw away your best source of indirect promotion.

PR Firms

One of the first things Apple did in 1984 when it wanted to launch its Macintosh was to hire a public relations firm. It hired Regis McKenna, one of the best PR firms in Silicon Valley, which has remained their PR firm since then. All of the major computer companies hire PR firms, and there are very good reasons for doing so. Your company may be seen as more credible by the press if it deals with you through a PR firm. PR firms live or die on their reputations with the press. PR firms don't contact the press unless they have a story. The PR agents are the experts in the field and know how to "package" a company for the press and media. Most importantly, the press usually returns the calls of a good PR agent.

The cost of hiring a PR firm or agent will depend on how much you choose to use them. Larger companies that spend millions on advertising spend anywhere from 1 percent to 10 percent of their ad budget on their PR firms. Even so, they often receive about the same amount of newsprint, airtime, or the same amount of value from each. Considering the added credibility that editorials bring, PR can be extremely cost-effective. Medium-sized companies should count on spending about the same amount on PR as they would pay a top salesperson. If you've hired the right PR company, you should be able to improve your bottom line measurably.

As well, PR firms should be able to obtain key information about your competition. If you know when your competition is going to announce a particular software product, you can undercut their impact by coming out with a press release of your own.

Trade Shows and Promotions

Every year, thousands of trade shows take place on a local, regional, and national level. Most of the biggest shows take place in the USA, Japan, and Germany, but shows of considerable size also occur in several other countries. Trade shows are more important to the multimedia industry than to most other industries. That's because *everyone* attends multimedia-related trade shows. Consumers, press, and industry giants all come together at Comdex, MacWorld, and any of the smaller or regional computer shows.

The major shows are expensive if you want to rent a booth. You can cut down the cost of booth space by leveraging off your relationship with a major hardware manufacturer or software distributor. These major companies always buy a booth at the big shows. They often offer cut rate – or even free – booth space to developers whose products can best showcase the technology of the major company. The small developer benefits by the reduced cost and by the association with Apple, IBM, Compton's, or one of the other multimedia giants.

If you can't get into one of these booths, the major shows are relatively inexpensive to attend. If you are a small developer, the information you get out of the major shows may not be effective for your needs. In fact, you will probably get more information than you can possibly process. The leads that you will find are usually not targeted. You may want to concentrate on local or regional shows or, even better, shows that are focused on your particular types of products. At least one show company, MacWorld's Mitch Hall and Associates, has announced cut-rate show space for "emerging companies."

For a complete list of trade shows, consult Chapter 15.

Don't think that you have to go to a computer show to sell your product. Remember, multimedia is flashy and impressive, but only when it is unique. In a computer or multimedia show, your multimedia aspects will not be unique. However, at a bridal show, an automotive show, or a dental convention, your product will get some press. Obviously your product has to be related to the specific concerns of the trade show. At a bridal show, you can demonstrate your wedding organizational software or perhaps Photo-CD product. At an automotive show or dental convention, present your template product for mechanics or dental offices, respectively.

If you are a speaker at a trade show, you might be asked to give a press quote. Prepare for this. Do not present a long, rambling comment. Make a provocative, punchy quote that translates well to consumers. Prepare a few one-line quotes concerning various story focuses that writers can easily incorporate into their articles. Your job here is to act as an industry consultant or spokesperson. Your job is not to sell your product or service overtly. Quotes like "Our product is far more useful/fun/better designed than the competition" are not likely to be used. It is impossible to verify such quotes and they look like the self-serving advertising they are.

Don't expect sponsorship or advertising dollars by influencing editorial staff. Most editors and reporters are extremely wary of compromising journalistic integrity. They do not want to appear biased. After all, their reputation as being objective is the only criterion that gives them credibility, and therefore power. The only exception may occur when the owner or publisher is somehow connected to the product. Even so, this pull will get you in the door but will not necessarily get you a resounding review.

Making Press Relations Equal Sales

People believe reviews and articles more than advertising. These reviews and articles are supposed to be objectively written by truth-seeking reporters. This makes the reader value press articles more than advertising. You can't tell the press what to write. However, you can positively influence it by providing professional, well-written press releases that translate into ready-made articles or reviews.

Many fledgling computer companies want to treat the press as their personal public relations department. Respect the press for the job it does. Your press release is probably not the most important thing on the editor's mind. No editor, assistant editor, staff reporter or freelancer wants to be hounded about a story. Don't call anyone from the press more than once a day unless you are playing telephone tag. Be aware that reporters may be on extremely tight deadlines, and that many freelancers work after hours. Make yourself available to the press at its convenience.

Recognize that the press may not wish to publish a story about you or your company when you really need it. You may want advance hype about an upcoming multimedia event in which you are involved, but the press will only review it *after* the fact. Don't get angry and burn your bridges. Give the press a good story after the fact, but add in some promotional material for your next event. When you're just starting out, any mention in the press – even if it is late – is a bonus. Establishing press relations takes time. Look at it as an investment for your future.

Chapter 13

Summing Up

According to Infonetics Research, nearly half of all installed microcomputers will be able to handle full-motion video by 1997, which will allow multimedia to become a part of everyone's life. A Dataquest survey of 200 large companies using multimedia found that two-thirds use multimedia for business presentations, over 60 percent use it for training, and one-quarter use multimedia for video-conferencing. As we discussed in Chapters 9 and 11, the education and home markets are expected to have even greater growth rates and percentages, as shown by an 82 percent annual growth rate in the plans to purchase. The multimedia market is growing as multimedia becomes a standard resource for the business, educational, and general consumer.

There is a great deal to think about when developing a multimedia product or project, when investing in multimedia ventures, or when running a multimedia business. The information in this book is only part of what you will need to know to succeed in a multimedia business. You can use this book to start out on the right path and as a guide along the road to success. The most important thing to remember is to plan ahead.

The Basics

To be successful in the multimedia industry, follow a few basic steps and create your own mark within this framework. To start a venture you need a great idea, money, perseverance, talent, and luck. A great idea is not only something *you* consider good but something many people consider *so* good that they must have it. Your product or project should entertain, educate, or help a large market do business. It must be something that you are both capable of and comfortable producing. It is important not to lose track of your own abilities and interests.

Don't underestimate how much money you will need to create and successfully bring to market a multimedia product or project. Software, content, and talent all cost considerable amounts of money. There *will* be problems, bugs, viruses, delays, in-house fights and posturing, revisions, and company and project restructuring. All of this will cost time and money.

Even the smoothest-running venture will require many hours of design, programming, entry, editing, and proofing. If there are certain technological or artistic elements that you do not understand or with which you have little experience, you will have to contract out the appropriate talent. Bringing in an outside element, like a contractor, means entering a potential wild card into your pack. You have to know that your project will stay on budget so you have to know that it will stay within projected timelines. Before you hire a contractor, get a solid time quote and make him or her stick to it.

You may not personally have the talent you require for your project. The multimedia industry represents the convergence of a number of different elements so your product or project may require the convergence of a number of different talented people.

In the multimedia industry, luck means having the right product or project at the right place at the right time. You can increase your luck by keeping watch over the multimedia marketplace, keeping up with trends, and developing good contacts.

Plan Ahead

As we've stressed throughout this book, planning is imperative to succeeding in business. The many diverse elements comprising multimedia can make for chaos in the studio and the boardroom or they can make magic on-screen and in your wallet. Planning makes all the difference. Have a well-written business plan before you go for financing. Draw up a marketing plan before you start developing your product. Obtain all necessary consents, releases, and waivers for all your content before you integrate it into your project. Make sure you understand every part of a contract before you sign, and make sure you get a signature on every contract you need.

Prepare for distribution before you code. Start looking for distributors at the same time you interview team members for your project. The old adage "It's not what you know, it's who you know" rings true in the multimedia industry. Contacts in the industry can be your most valuable commodity. You have to figure out who can help you in your business and then spend time cultivating these business relationships. This may sound mercenary but, in fact, it's simply good business.

Fully analyze and outline your objectives, strategies, and tactics before starting your business. As well, periodically review your company to ensure that it is fulfilling its objectives, strategies, and tactics, and to ensure that the objectives you originally decided upon still apply. Keep good financial records. And get advice from professionals you understand and trust. The best lawyers, accountants, marketing consultants, and other professionals should be able to get results but they should also be able to take you through the process. Seek out professionals who provide you with complete reports on their activities without using jargon. These professionals work for *you* and should provide you with valuable enlightenment. After all, it's your business and you should have at least a basic understanding of how all aspects of the business operate.

How to Read the Market and Read about the Market

The multimedia industry is rapidly growing and changing and it will continue to do so. You have to keep informed about everything that affects your company, your competition, your distributors, the developers of complementary products, and all multimedia industry giants. You also have to keep informed about your customers.

The trick is to keep ahead of the market, but not too far ahead. The most important point to remember in marketing is to know your market. Anticipating your market can make you extremely successful only if your market is ready for your innovation. However, riding the wave of a particular technological trend can be dangerous since technology becomes obsolete faster and faster these days.

In Chapter 15, we outline many of the sources available to help you stay up-to-date in the multimedia industry.

The best way to ensure that you remain in business is to develop products with longevity. By using multimedia as a *support* for your product instead of as a focus, you can market timeless content with the latest techniques. The result should be success.

The Future for Multimedia

Today multimedia is an industry unto itself, but in the future there will be no multimedia industry as we know it today. Instead, multimedia will become integrated into everyday life. Multimedia products will continue to grow in market share. Multimedia will become such an integral part of entertainment, education, business, and life that we will take it for granted. Just like desktop publishing and database management – once considered fringe or separate markets within the computer industry – multimedia will be absorbed into the mainstream. Now's the time to establish yourself as a multimedia player.

Chapter 14

Sample Documents

To understand the documents surrounding the business of multimedia you should have an idea of what they contain. There are numerous ways to write most business documents. However, there is generally a suggested format from which to begin.

The following sample documents represent two of the documents you will – or should – work with most. News releases should be sent out on a regular basis. A business plan is the contact paper between the developer and the venture capitalist or investor, and can make or break your financing and your project.

The documents provided here are for reference only. They are intentionally general and in their most basic form. They are not intended to replace the work of professionals as they have not been specifically designed for your projects. The problem with using standard forms is that they are not written with your company and project in mind. *Always* get professional advice before using *any* document.

News Release

SECRETS OF MULTIMEDIA BUSINESS EXPLAINED IN NEW BOOK

APPLE AND ADDISON-WESLEY PUBLISH
MAKING MONEY WITH MULTIMEDIA

SAN FRANCISCO, California — October 2, 1994 — Multimedia developers who need business training quickly can benefit from expert advice and insight with a new book from Apple and Addison-Wesley. *Making Money with Multimedia* explains the business side of the multimedia industry with specific advice for developers, investors, and in-house professionals. If you are involved with development, distribution, or use of CD-ROMs, kiosks, business presentations, multimedia games, video conferencing, electronic books and magazines, or any of the far-reaching uses of multimedia, this book will be an invaluable resource.

The authors David Rosen and Caryn Mladen are business professionals working in the multimedia and computer industry. David Rosen is a respected marketing consultant who has worked with such technology giants and innovators as Apple Computer, Inc., Siemens Nixdorf Information Systems, and Coopers & Lybrand. Caryn Mladen is a technology lawyer specializing in multimedia and developing technologies. Both have written and been quoted in numerous industry publications and general interest magazines, as well as have spoken frequently at conferences, symposiums, colleges, and trade shows on issues related to multimedia.

"This book had to be written. Until now there was no one source for those interested in taking a multimedia project to market or investing in multimedia," says Satjiv Chahil, Vice President and General Manager, New Media Division,
Apple Computer, Inc. "Sponsoring *Making Money with Multimedia* demonstrates Apple's commitment to the exploding multimedia industry. This book was written with the advice of expert consultants and staff both from Apple and the other leaders in the multimedia industry."

Making Money with Multimedia shows developers how to bring their multimedia products to market – on time and on budget. The book also helps investors understand the workings of a multimedia company, and gives them tools to assess the viability of possible multimedia investments. With chapters on marketing, sales, finance, and distribution, the book provides a previously neglected focus on the all important business side of the multimedia industry. With a detailed list of sources including venture capitalists, distributors, trade shows, books, and magazines, *Making Money with Multimedia* also acts as an invaluable reference guide to anyone in the multimedia industry.

"Orders are already pouring in from every English-speaking country in the world," says Heather Rignanesi, General Manager Trade, Addison-Wesley Publishers Limited. With offices in Menlo Park, New York, Toronto, Singapore, Amsterdam, Paris, Sydney, and other cities throughout the world, Addison-Wesley is renowned for publishing technical, business, and legal books for the high-technology sector. "Addison-Wesley and Apple are working together again to promote the
convergence of different industries and businesses which parallel the convergence of technologies today. With its straight-forward approach to business and technology, *Making Money with Multimedia* was an obvious choice for both companies."

Making Money with Multimedia is now being sent to all members of the Apple Multimedia Program (AMP) as one of the many benefits of program membership. Apple is actively sponsoring a variety of books and materials on multimedia, creating complete, detailed, useful resources for developers and anyone in the business. Apple has been a leader in the development and distribution of new media products. For information on AMP call 408-974-4897.

Making Money with Multimedia was released today and is available in bookstores across the country and around the world for US$15.95. To order your copy call 1-800-387-8028.

For more information contact:

Katy Boos
Apple Computer, Inc.
(408) 974-4451

Heather Rignanesi
Addison-Wesley Publishers Limited.
(416) 447-5101

Apple is a registered trademark of Apple Computer, Inc.

Business Plan

The following is a summarized business plan for a multimedia company specializing in the development of CD-ROM titles for the over-50 age market. We have created it as an example of a potential project to showcase the business plan. We must stress that we do not advocate the project or activities listed in the business plan and that the information may not be correct. The information was constructed to showcase the format of a fictitious multimedia business plan. For the purposes of the example, the specific subject is irrelevant. Space limitations prevent us from going into the detail that such a business plan requires. For example, we have not included an executive summary because this business plan contains only the basic information that one would find in an executive summary. Condensing it further would not be effective. Use the following plan as a framework or blueprint for your own particular business and projects.

For a fuller and more complete examination of business plans, review business plan software and books, including some of those listed in Chapter 15.

BUSINESS PLAN

This plan has been designed by the executives of ANY Multimedia Corp. ("ANY"). Its purpose is two-fold. First to detail the present situation of ANY, and second to establish a plan for the future based on increased financing.

FINANCING GOAL

Amount:	$1,000,000.00
Project:	*The Body Over 50*
	A series of CD-ROMs about health for people over 50.
Terms:	Sale of 50 percent of projected revenues.
Present Assets:	$200,000.00 in cash, equipment, intellectual property, and accounts receivable.
Executive Officers:	Amy Green and Moe Green

Statement of Purpose

ANY is committed to the development of multimedia CD-ROM titles for the over-50 age market. Currently ANY has two completed titles. *Golfing with the Masters* is presently in distribution and has shipped over 50,000 discs worldwide. ANY is presently preparing *Estate Planning for You* for domestic distribution. Several other discs are in the design and development stage. Detailed plans for these discs can be obtained upon signage of the enclosed non-disclosure agreement. With further financing, ANY will be able to expand its marketing activities and develop a series of titles based on health concerns of the over-50 market.

Business Environment

The over-50 age market has been the last to respond to the explosion of multimedia products on the market. Fictitious Research Inc. shows that CD-ROM drives exist in only 10 percent of households with people over 50, representing half of the average percentage for all households. However, market penetration in the over-50 age group is growing at a higher rate than that in the average household. The market has not become over-saturated with products specifically aimed at this market. The market has a relatively high level of disposable wealth and time for leisure activities. There is tremendous scope for the exploitation of this market if approached effectively.

Ownership Structure

ANY Multimedia is a corporation incorporated under the laws of the State of California. Its shares are fully and equally owned by the two founding partners, Moe Green and Amy Green. There are no other equity participant owners at present.

Management Team

Both Moe and Amy have experience in creating interactive multimedia productions. Moe gained experience in this industry through 10 years of work at XYZ Television Studios in several management positions such as Line Producer of Daytime Television and Director of Daytime

Programming. Amy has had various jobs in the film industry including Producer and Assistant Producer of both documentary feature films and made-for-television specials. Both are over 50 years of age and are very active in sports and charitable activities within their community. Moe holds a Bachelor's degree in Business from City College and Amy holds a Master of Education from State University and a Ph.D. from Concordance in Seniors Education Techniques. Her doctoral thesis was "How seniors can lead more active lives through sports and technology." Moe and Amy lead their staff of expert programmers, designers, artists, researchers, and writers.

Project Plan

In the past, ANY has been extremely pro-active in obtaining content and leveraging relationships with distributors. For the intended series of CD-ROM titles, ANY has brought negotiations to the final stage, requiring less than 2 percent of the budget for future R&D. The contracts are ready to be signed, once financing has been obtained. Upon receiving sufficient financing, ANY will execute contracts for the needed content, distribution, and marketing. Due to the well-organized nature of the existing software developed in-house, ANY's programming staff will be able to simply and quickly integrate the content into the software.

Each title will require approximately four months in development and programming. During this time, storyboarding, content development, content licensing (as applicable), graphic design, and cover art will be undertaken at pre-established intervals in the development process. ANY will initiate marketing activities in conjunction with established print guidelines for monthly, weekly, and daily trade publications. ANY will spend approximately 20 percent of the total budget on sales and marketing. Near the end of the development cycle, ANY will contact its established distributors to explain fully the widening of ANY's product range and to set up the distribution mechanism.

Marketing Plan

Based on ANY's extensive experience in marketing to the over-50 age group, ANY believes that the project discs will sell to this relatively affluent demograph. ANY's market research shows that this audience can be reached through a series of traditional and non-traditional methods. The traditional methods include advertising in seniors magazines, mailing to ANY's installed-base, sending ANY's marketing representative to demonstrate the product at local seniors television current affairs programs, as well as among seniors groups and associations. The non-traditional methods include CD-ROM infomercials, point of sale displays at medical cross-marketing venues, and providing informational kiosks with the product installed at high traffic areas such as shopping malls, large pharmacies, and hospitals.

Research and Development Plan

ANY is working with staff at XYZ Hospital of San Francisco, California, to determine the needs and interests of the over-50 market in issues of health and well-being. XYZ is willing to lend its name to the series of discs in exchange for proper credit and access rights to the series of discs. No monetary remuneration need be provided. Through their industry connections in the television industry, Amy and Moe Green have arranged contracts to secure content for the series of multimedia products in development.

ANY uses search and presentation engines (multimedia programming tools to find and present information on a CD-ROM) that were developed in-house. Both these engines have proven successful for the first two discs. ANY's customer feedback on search and presentation results has been extremely positive, indicating that the engines are an excellent base for future products to this market. ANY is continuing to improve and develop these engines based on expert feedback.

Two important features of the engines are the E-Z-Read™ and E-Z-Hear™ components. E-Z-Read allows the user of the CD to magnify the text on demand and to modify the lighting and other visual factors quickly and easily. E-Z-Hear allows users to adjust pitch, frequency and other auditory factors on demand. Both of these components are especially attractive to users whose eyesight and hearing may be diminishing or fluctuating over time. These components allow for better enjoyment of ANY's products. Both E-Z-Read and E-Z-Hear are trademarked by ANY and patents are pending in the United States.

STAFF AND LOCATIONAL PLAN

Dr. Goode Doktor, the Chief of Geriatric Medicine at First Hospital of San Francisco, California, has committed to provide his name and content expertise for the series of health-based CD-ROMs in exchange for a 5 percent royalty on the net sales of the series. His reputation should prove a great help in marketing and selling the series. ANY has four full-time employees working in programming, graphic design, interface animation, and rendering. As well, ANY has well-established relationships with a large number of freelance multimedia contractors who are willing to join the team as required. Hiring these freelance contractors is dependent upon obtaining suitable financial support.

All development work is completed at ANY's studio and office at 12345 Main Street, Anytown, California, 95555.

Financial Plan

Budget Assumptions – Your Body Over 50 – Year 1

Company confidential
Assume: margin per disc sold: $30

	Month 1	Month 2	Month 3	Month 4	Month 5 (Rollout)
Sales - quantity	0	0	0	0	3,500
Sales (margin per disc X quantity)	$0	$0	$0	$0	$105,000
Cost of Goods Sold					
Raw Materials (disc manufacture)	$0	$0	$0	$10,000	$0
Labor (packing and labelling)	$0	$0	$0	$1,000	$500
Total COGS	$0	$0	$0	$11,000	$500
Sales & Marketing Expense					
Advertising	$0	$0	$0	$10,000	$10,000
Rollout	$0	$0	$0	$0	$15,000
Collateral	$0	$0	$0	$2,500	$2,500
Promotion	$0	$0	$0	$2,500	$2,500
Salaries	$0	$5,000	$5,000	$5,000	$6,500
Trade Shows	$0	$0	$0	$0	$2,000
Travel	$0	$0	$0	$0	$1,000
Total Sales & Marketing Expenses	$0	$5,000	$5,000	$20,000	$39,500
Research & Development (R&D)					
Consulting	$2,000	$0	$0	$0	$0
Leased Equipment	$500	$500	$500	$500	$500
R&D Salary Expense	$5,000	$5,000	$5,000	$5,000	$2,500
R&D Materials Expense	$250	$250	$250	$250	$250
Total R&D Expenses	$7,750	$5,750	$5,750	$5,750	$3,250
General & Administrative Expenses					
Accounting	$250	$250	$250	$250	$250
Administrative Salaries (pro-rata)	$1,000	$1,000	$1,000	$1,000	$1,000
Bad Debt Expense	$0	$0	$0	$0	$2,000
Depreciation Expense	$250	$250	$250	$250	$250
Insurance Expense	$150	$150	$150	$150	$150
Legal Fees	$10,000	$5,000	$5,000	$5,000	$1,000
Licenses & Permits	$100	$100	$100	$100	$100
Office Expenses (pro-rata)	$1,000	$1,000	$1,000	$1,000	$1,000
Office Rental (pro-rata)	$200	$200	$200	$200	$200
Taxes (non-Income Tax)	$100	$100	$100	$100	$100
Telephone	$250	$250	$250	$250	$250
Utilities	$200	$200	$200	$200	$200
Total G&A Expenses	$13,500	$8,500	$8,500	$8,500	$6,500
Total Expenses	$21,250	$19,250	$19,250	$45,250	$49,750
Monthly Profit (Loss)	($21,250)	($19,250)	($19,250)	($45,250)	$55,250
Cummulative Profit (Loss)	($21,250)	($40,500)	($59,750)	($105,000)	($49,750)

Month 6	Month 7	Month 8	Month 9	Month 10	Month 11	Month 12	Total
4,500	4,500	5,500	6,500	7,500	8,500	9,500	50,000
$135,000	$135,000	$165,000	$195,000	$225,000	$255,000	$285,000	$1,500,000
$10,000	$0	$10,000	$0	$10,000	$0	$10,000	$50,000
$1,000	$500	$1,000	$500	$1,000	$500	$1,000	$7,000
$11,000	$500	$11,000	$500	$11,000	$500	$11,000	$57,000
$10,000	$10,000	$10,000	$10,000	$10,000	$10,000	$10,000	$90,000
$0	$0	$0	$0	$0	$0	$0	$15,000
$0	$2,500	$0	$2,500	$0	$2,500	$0	$12,500
$2,500	$2,500	$2,500	$2,500	$2,500	$2,500	$2,500	$22,500
$6,500	$6,500	$6,500	$6,500	$6,500	$6,500	$6,500	$67,000
$0	$2,000	$0	$2,000	$0	$2,000	$0	$8,000
$500	$1,000	$500	$1,000	$500	$0	$500	$5,000
$19,500	$24,500	$19,500	$24,500	$19,500	$23,500	$19,500	$220,000
$0	$0	$0	$0	$0	$0	$0	$2,000
$500	$0	$0	$0	$0	$0	$0	$3,000
$1,000	$1,000	$1,000	$0	$1,000	$0	$1,000	$27,500
$250	$250	$250	$0	$250	$0	$250	$2,500
$1,750	$1,250	$1,250	$0	$1,250	$0	$1,250	$35,000
$250	$250	$250	$250	$250	$250	$250	$3,000
$1,000	$1,000	$1,000	$1,000	$1,000	$1,000	$1,000	$12,000
$2,000	$2,000	$2,000	$2,000	$2,000	$2,000	$2,000	$16,000
$250	$250	$250	$250	$250	$250	$250	$3,000
$150	$150	$150	$150	$150	$150	$150	$1,800
$1,000	$1,000	$1,000	$1,000	$1,000	$1,000	$1,000	$33,000
$100	$100	$100	$100	$100	$100	$100	$1,200
$1,000	$1,000	$1,000	$1,000	$1,000	$1,000	$1,000	$12,000
$200	$200	$200	$200	$200	$200	$200	$2,400
$100	$100	$100	$100	$100	$100	$100	$1,200
$250	$250	$250	$250	$250	$250	$250	$3,000
$200	$200	$200	$200	$200	$200	$200	$2,400
$6,500	$6,500	$6,500	$6,500	$6,500	$6,500	$6,500	$91,000
$38,750	$32,750	$38,250	$31,500	$38,250	$30,500	$38,250	$403,000
$96,250	$102,250	$126,750	$163,500	$186,750	$224,500	$246,750	$1,097,000
$46,500	$148,750	$275,500	$439,000	$625,750	$850,250	$1,097,000	

Complete this worksheet for every company you investigate in your search for the ideal business partner.

Marketing Worksheet

Company Name: _____   Contact: _____
Address: _____   Tilte: _____
City, State/Prov: _____   Zip/Postal: _____
Phone: _____   Fax: _____
e-Mail Address: _____   Other: _____

Target Market: Consumer, Corporate, Education, Government, Vertical: _____
_____

Geographics Covered: _____
_____

Type of Company: Distributor, Publisher, Retailer, Developer, Mail Order
_____
_____

Submission Process: _____
_____
_____

Payment/Royalty Structure: _____
_____
_____

Other Comments: _____
_____
_____
_____

There are many more documents that you will see in everyday business. We have not included those that change drastically by jurisdiction and project. Have your lawyer draw up standard licensing agreements for the licensing of content and software as applicable to your project. Similarly, a lawyer and accountant should be involved in drawing up partnership agreements or shareholders' agreements and other corporate documents. The money you spend on their fees is more than worth the hassles you will avoid.

Chapter 15

Sources

Mention of any sources including distributors, venture capitalists, magazines, books, and other sources in these lists is for informational purposes only and constitutes neither an endorsement nor a recommendation by the Authors, Apple Computer, Inc., or Addison-Wesley-Publishers Limited, who assume no responsibility with regard to your activities. This chapter does not represent a complete listing of any of the referenced sources.

Distributors

NORTH AMERICA

Starting with the big three in North America: Figures following telephone numbers are the estimated sales in US dollars. We have not included the sales figures for smaller publishers and distributors because most of these are privately held companies that will not release their figures. All companies listed are strictly distributors unless otherwise indicated.

Ingram Micro
1600 East St. Andrew Place, P.O. Box 25125
Santa Ana, CA, USA, 92799-5125
714-566-1000
$4 billion: 1993; over $5 billion: 1994

Merisel
300 Continental Boulevard
El Segundo, CA, USA, 90245
1-800-MERISEL
$3 billion: 1993; $4 billion: 1994

Tech Data
5350 Tech Data Drive
Clearwater, FL, USA, 38620
1-800-327-8931
$1.5 billion: 1993; $2 billion: 1994

Small and Medium-Sized Distributors:
Baker & Taylor Software
3850 Royal Avenue
Simi Valley, CA, USA, 93063
800-775-4100

D&H Distributing
2525 North 7th Street
Harrisburg, PA USA, 17110
1-800-877-1200

Educorp (also a Publisher and Developer)
7434 Trade Street
San Diego, CA, USA, 92121-2410
619-536-9999

Kenfill Distribution
16745 Saticoy Street
Van Nuys, CA, USA, 91406
818-785-1181

MacWarehouse/MicroWarehouse (Mail-order Distributor)
PO Box 3013
1720 Oak Street
Lakewood, NJ, USA, 08701-3013
1-800-255-6227/908-370-3801

One Stop Micro
524 Prospect Avenue
Little Silver, NJ, USA, 07739
1-800-248-9666

EMJ
Courier address: RR#6, Highway #24
Guelph, ON, Canada, N1H 6J3
Postal address: P.O. Box 1012
Guelph, ON, Canada, N1H 6N1
1-800-265-7212/510-837-2444

Ingram Micro Canada
230 Barmac Drive
Weston, ON, Canada, M9L 2Z3
416-740-9404

Merisel Canada
731 Millway Avenue
Concord, ON, Canada, L4K 3S8
905-738-3920

EUROPE

Computers Unlimited (also a Retailer)
No. 2 The Business Centre
Colindeep Lane
London, UK, NW9 6DU
44-81-200-8282

Euro-CD
13 Cité Voltaire
75011 Paris, France
40-09-80-30

Frontline Distribution
Intec
1 Wade Road, Basingstoke
Hants, UK, RG24 0NE
44-256-463344

GEM Distribution Company
Lovet Road, The Pinnacles
Harlow, Essex, UK, CM19 5TB
44-279-442-842

Principal Distribution Ltd.
1 Roundwood Avenue
Stockley Park, Uxbridge, UK, UB11 IAY
081-813-5656

AUSTRALIA

Dataflow Computer Services P/L
15 Merton Street
Zetland, New South Wales
2017, Australia
612-310-2020

Merisel Australia
4 Serius Road
P.O. Box 274
Lane Cove, New South Wales
2006, Australia
612-882-8888

Tech Pacific
77 Dunning Avenue
Rosebury, New South Wales
2018, Australia
612-697-8666

ASIA

Asia CD Ltd.
12F, Hong Kong Arts Centre
2 Harbour Road
Wanchai, Hong Kong
852-824-0781

Media Exchange
2F Heiwadai Bld. 1-1-1
Otemon, Chuo-ku, Fukuoka 810 Japan
092-715-6133

Oki Software, Packaged Software Division
Nakano Spring Building
Shibaura 4-11-17
Minato-ku, Tokyo 108 Japan
03-3454-7831

Catena Corp., Packaged Software Publishing Center
10-24-2 Shiomi
Kouto-ku, Tokyo 135 Japan
03-3615-9001
or
1050 E. Duane Avenue, Suite #C
Sunnyvale, CA 94086 USA
408-746-3615

Focal Point Computer, Inc.
Minoru Akuhara
Mita SK Bldg., 2nd Floor
1-3-34 Mita
Minato-ku, Tokyo 108 Japan
03-5484-0140

Swire Transtech Ltd.
Swire House
14, Ichibancho, Chiyoda-ku, Tokyo 102 Japan
03-3230-9177

Major Consumer Market Developers, Publishers, and Distributors

Aris Entertainment – Developer, Publisher, and Distributor
310 Washington Boulevard, Suite 100, Marina del Ray, CA, USA, 90292,
Tel: 310-821-0234. Market: business presentations and games.

Baker & Taylor Software – Distributor
3850 Royal Avenue, Simi Valley, CA, USA, 93063, Tel: 800-775-4100.
Market: diverse.

Blockbuster Entertainment Co. – Retailer
One Blockbuster Plaza, 200 South Andrews Avenue, Fort Lauderdale,
FL, USA, 33301, Tel: 305-832-3265. Market: entertainment and general
CD-ROM rentals.

Brøderbund Software, Inc. – Developer and Publisher
500 Redwood Boulevard, Novato, CA, USA, 94948, Tel: 415-382-4617.
Market: diverse; concentrating on edutainment and children's
educational titles.

Cambrix Publishing – Developer, Publisher, and Distributor
6269 Variel Avenue, Suite B, Woodland Hills, CA, USA, 91367,
Tel: 818-992-8484. Market: edutainment and education.

Claris Clear Choice – Developer and Publisher
5201 Patrick Henry Drive, P.O. Box 58168, Santa Clara, CA, USA, 95052,
Tel: 408-987-7000/800-325-2747. Market: entertainment and
educational titles.

Compton's New Media – Developer, Publisher and Distributor
2320 Camino Vida Roble, Carlsbad, CA, USA, 92009-1504,
Tel: 619-929-2500. Market: reference, games, entertainment,
and educational titles.

Corel Systems – Developer, Publisher, and Distributor
1600 Carling Avenue, Ottawa, ON, Canada, K1Z 8R7, Tel: 800-772-6735/613-728-8200. Market: photographic clip art and application software.

Creative Multimedia Corporation – Developer and Publisher
514 N.W. 11th Avenue, Suite 203, Portland, OR, USA, 97209,
Tel: 503-241-4351. Market: diverse; entertainment, educational, and general consumer markets.

Discis Knowledge Research, Inc. – Developer, Publisher, and Distributor
90 Sheppard Avenue East, 7th floor, Willowdale, ON, Canada, M2N 3A1, 800-567-4321/416-250-6537. Market: electronic books and games, especially children's market.

Disney Software – Developer and Publisher
500 South Buena Vista Street, Burbank, CA, USA, 91521-6385,
Tel: 818-973-4015. Disney Software is a subsidiary of The Walt Disney Company. Market: Interactive children's books and games.

Electronic Arts – Publisher and Distributor
1450 Fashion Island Boulevard, San Mateo, CA, USA, 94404-2064,
Tel: 415-571-7171 (extension 1670 for product submission form).
Market: edutainment and education.

Educorp – Developer, Publisher, and Distributor
7434 Trade Street, San Diego, CA, USA, 92121, Tel: 619-536-9999.
Market: educational and informational multimedia products.

Euro-CD – Distributor
13 Cité Voltaire, 75011 Paris, France, 33-1-40-09-80-30. Market: diverse; anything North American in Europe.

Grolier Electronic Publishing, Inc. – Developer and Publisher
Sherman Turnpike, Danbury, CT, USA, 06816, 800-356-5590/
203-797-3530. Market: reference.

Philips Interactive Media of America – Developer, Publisher, and Distributor
11111 Santa Monica Boulevard, Los Angeles, CA, USA, 90025,
Tel: 310-445-5000. Market: diverse; entertainment relating to sports, music and children's entertainment.

Time Warner Interactive – Developer and Publisher
2210 West Olive Avenue, Burbank, CA, USA, 91506, Tel: 818-955-9999. Market: reference and entertainment.

The Voyager Company – Developer, Publisher, and Distributor
1351 Pacific Coast Highway, Santa Monica, CA, USA, 90401,
Tel: 310-451-1383. Market: entertainment, educational, and general consumer markets.

Wayzata Technology, Inc. – Developer and Publisher
2515 East Highway 2, Grand Rapids, MN, USA, 55744, Tel: 800-735-7321/ 218-326-0597. Market: diverse; entertainment, educational, and general consumer markets.

Xiphias – Developer and Publisher
Helms Hall, 8758 Venice Boulevard, Los Angeles, CA, USA, 90034,
Tel: 310-841-2790. Market: reference.

Venture Capitalists

Before contacting a VC firm, review the material in Chapters 3 and 6. VC firms are private companies interested in the bottom line. In most circumstances, VC firms will contact those companies that interest them and not bother with the many solicitations by eager developers.

Accel Partners
1 Enbarcadero Center, Suite 3820
San Francisco, CA, USA, 94111
415-989-5656

Asset Management
2275 East Bayshore Road, Suite 150
Palo Alto, CA, USA, 94303
415-494-7400

AT&T Ventures
11 Eagle Rock Avenue, Suite 130
East Hanover, NJ, USA, 07936
201-952-1470

Battery Ventures
200 Portland Street
Boston, MA, USA, 02114
617-367-1011

Bessemer Venture Partners
3000 Sand Hill Road, Building 3, Suite 225
Menlo Park, CA, USA, 94025
415-854-2200

Burr, Egan, Deleage
1 Post Office Square, Suite 3800
Boston, MA, USA, 02109
617-482-8020

Canaan Partners
2884 Sand Hill Road, Suite 115
Menlo Park, CA, USA, 94025
415-854-8092

Coral Group
60 South 6th Street, Suite 3510
Minneapolis, MN, USA, 55402
612-335-8666

Draper Associates
400 Seaport Court, Suite 250
Port of Redwood City, CA, USA, 94063
415-599-9000

Institutional Venture Partners
3000 Sand Hill Road, Building 2, Suite 290
Menlo Park, CA, USA, 94025
415-854-0132

Kleiner, Perkins, Caulfield & Buyers
2750 Sand Hill Road
Menlo Park, CA, USA, 94025
415-233-2750

Matrix Partners
1 International Place, Suite 3250
Boston, MA, USA, 02110
617-345-6740

Mayfield Fund
2800 Sand Hill Road, Suite 250
Menlo Park, CA, USA, 94025
415-854-5560

Menlo Ventures
3000 Sand Hill Road, Building 4, Suite 1000
Menlo Park, CA, USA, 94025
415-854-8540

Merrill, Pickard, Anderson & Eyre
2480 Sand Hill Road, Suite 200
Menlo Park, CA, USA, 94025
415-854-8600

Mohr, Davidow Ventures
3000 Sand Hill Road, Building 1, Suite 240
Menlo Park, CA, USA, 94025
415-854-7236

New Enterprise Associates (NEA)
3000 Sand Hill Road, Building 4, Suite 235
Menlo Park, CA, USA, 94025
415-854-2660

Sequoia Capital
3000 Sand Hill Road, Building 4, Suite 280
Menlo Park, CA, USA, 94025
415-854-3927

Sigma Partners
2884 Sand Hill Road, Suite 121
Menlo Park, CA, USA, 94025
415-854-1300

Summit Partners
One Boston Place
Boston, MA, USA, 02108
617-742-5500

Trademark Information

The Assistant Secretary and Commissioner of Patents & Trademarks
Trademark Examining Division
Washington, D.C., U.S.A. 20231

The Registrar of Trade-marks
Consumer and Corporate Affairs Canada
50 Victoria Street
Place du Portage, Tower 1
Hull, Quebec, Canada K1A 0C9

Copyright Information

The Public Information Office of the Copyright Office is in Washington, D.C. This office can be reached by telephone at 202-707-3000.

The Copyright Office operates a forms hotline telephone in Washington, D.C. and can be reached by telephoning 202-707-9100, or writing to Copyright Office, Library of Congress, USA, Washington, D.C. 20559.

Copyright and Industrial Design Branch
50 Victoria Street
Place du Portage, Tower 1
Hull, Quebec, Canada, K1A 0C9
819-997-1725

Licensing Content Sources

General Clearance Houses:
The Content Company
171 East 74th Street, 2nd Floor
New York, NY, USA, 10021
212-772-7363

Music Clearing House Ltd.
6605 Hollywood Blvd., Suite 200
Hollywood, CA, USA, 90028
213-469-3186

Total Clearance
P.O. Box 836
Mill Valley, CA, USA, 94942
415-445-5800

Stock Houses:

I Film and Video: Television and Movie studios can be approached directly. Otherwise the following stock houses can be approached.

Archive Films Stock Footage Library
530 West 25th Street
New York, NY, USA, 10001
800-886-3980/212-620-3980

Classic Images
1041 North Formosa Avenue
West Hollywood, CA, USA, 90046
213-850-2980

Energy Productions
12700 Ventura Boulevard
Studio City, CA, USA, 91604
818-508-1444

Filmbank
425 South Victory Boulevard
Burbank, CA, USA, 91502
818-841-9176

Image Bank Films
4526 Wilshire Boulevard
Los Angeles, CA, USA, 90010
213-930-0797
or
40 Eglinton Avenue East, Suite 307
Toronto, ON, Canada, M4P 3A8
416-322-8840

Imageways
412 West 48th Street
New York, NY, USA, 10036
800-862-1118

Mediacom
P.O. Box 36173
Richmond, VA, USA, 23235
804-794-0700

MPI Multimedia
5525 West 159th Street
Oak Forest, IL, USA, 60452
800-777-2223

II   PHOTOGRAPHY:

After Image, Inc.
6100 Wilshire Boulevard
Los Angeles, CA, USA, 90048
800-825-8899

Archive Photos
530 West 25th Street
New York, NY, USA, 10001
800-688-5656/212-594-8816

FPG International
32 Union Square East
New York, NY, USA, 10003
212-777-4210

Historical Picture Services, Inc.
921 West Van Buren, Suite 201
Chicago, IL, USA, 60607
312-346-0599

The Image Bank
4526 Wilshire Boulevard
Los Angeles, CA, USA, 90010
213-930-0797
or
111 Fifth Avenue
New York, NY, USA, 10003
212-529-6700
or
40 Eglinton Avenue East, Suite 307
Toronto, ON, Canada, M4P 3A8
416-322-8840

Photo Researchers, Inc.
60 East 56th Street
New York, NY, USA, 10022
800-833-9033/212-758-3420

Sharpshooters, Inc.
4950 Southwest 72nd Avenue, Suite 114
Miami, FL, USA, 33155
800-666-1266/305-666-1266

Stock Boston, Inc.
36 Gloucester Street
Boston, MA, USA, 02115
617-266-2300

SOURCES

Tony Stone Worldwide Stock Agency
6100 Wilshire Boulevard, Suite 240
Los Angeles, CA, USA, 90048
800-234-7880/213-938-1700
or
233 East Ontario Street, Suite 100
Chicago, IL, USA, 60611
800-234-7880/312-787-7880
or
161 Eglinton Avenue East, Suite 801
Toronto, ON, Canada, M4P 1J5
416-488-9495

Westlight
2223 South Carmelina Avenue
Los Angeles, CA, USA, 90064
800-872-7872/310-820-7077

III   SOUND AND MUSIC:

Associated Production Music
6255 Sunset Boulevard, Suite 820
Hollywood, CA, USA, 90028-9804
800-543-4276/213-461-3211

Capitol Production Music
6922 Hollywood Boulevard, Suite 718
Hollywood, CA, USA, 90028
213-461-2701

Hollywood Film Music Library
11684 Ventura Boulevard, Suite 850
Studio City, CA, USA, 91604
800-373-3256

Killer Tracks
6534 Sunset Boulevard
Hollywood, CA, USA, 90028
800-877-0078/213-957-4455

More Media
853 Broadway, Suite 1516
New York, NY, USA, 10003
212-677-8815

MPI Multimedia
5525 West 159th Street
Oak Forest, IL, USA, 60452
800-777-2223

Production Music Library Association
40 East 49th Street
New York, NY, USA, 10017
212-832-1098

Selected Sound Recorded Music Library
6777 Hollywood Boulevard, Suite 209
Hollywood, CA, USA, 90028
213-469-9910

Market Research Firms

Dataquest, Inc.
1290 Ridder Park Drive
San Jose, CA, USA, 95131-2398
408-437-8000

Freeman Associates, Inc.
311 East Carrillo Street
Santa Barbara, CA, USA, 93101
805-963-3853

Future Systems, Inc.
P.O. Box 26
Falls Church, VA, USA, 22040
800-323-3472

InfoTech
P.O. Box 150
Woodstock, VT, USA, 05091-0150
802-457-1037/802-457-1039

In-Stat, Inc.
7418 East Helm Drive
Scottsdale, AZ, USA, 85260-2418
602-483-4455

Inteco Corporation
110 Richards Avenue
Norwalk, CT, USA, 06852
203-866-4400

LINK Resources
19 Fifth Avenue
New York, NY, USA, 10003
212-627-1500

Market Vision
326 Pacheco Avenue, Suite 200
Santa Cruz, CA, USA, 95062
408-426-4400

Quality Education Data, Inc. (QED)
1600 Broadway, 12th Floor
Denver, CO, USA, 80202-4912
800-525-5811

SIMBA/Communications Trends, Inc.
213 Danbury Road
Box 7430
Wilton, CT, USA, 06897
203-834-0033

Magazines and Journals

Magazines are usually classified as general circulation and controlled (i.e., trade) magazines. Anyone can walk into a bookstore and purchase a general circulation magazine but controlled circulation magazines are restricted by invited subscription to members of a specific trade or profession. Generally speaking, trade magazines contain more useful information for multimedia developers than do those of general circulation. Trade magazines often highlight upcoming products and trends before they reach the general market. General magazines, on the other hand, are useful for judging the public's demand for a particular technology or product at a given time. We have included editorial contact numbers, where possible, to allow you to send out press releases to these magazines.

GENERAL CIRCULATION MAGAZINES

Apple Business (UK). EMAP Publishing, 34 Farrigdon Lane, London, UK, EC1R 3AU, Tel: 01 251 6222. Although dealing with the generalities of using Apple Macintosh computers in business, this magazine is useful for tracking the penetration of multimedia technologies within the UK.

Australian MacWorld. Published by IDG Communications, 88 Christie Street, St. Leonard's, NSW, Australia, 2065, Tel: 02-439-5123. Australian version of popular Mac-based news and reviews consumer magazine.

Sources

Business Week. Published weekly by McGraw-Hill Inc., 1221 Avenue of the Americas, NY, NY, USA, 10020. Many investors and managers read *Business Week* to spot upcoming trends and potential markets. You should too.

Byte's editorial and circulation offices are at One Phoenix Mill Lane, Peterborough, NH, USA, 03458, Tel: 603-924-9281. It is owned by media giant McGraw-Hill Inc. *Byte* advertises itself as "The Worldwide Computing Authority" and, as one of the oldest continuing computer magazines, lives up to its reputation. *Byte* uses a somewhat technical bits-and-bytes approach to product reviews so don't get intimidated if you feel it's over your head – it's written that way.

CD-ROM Multimedia Magazine. Editorial office 121 Westminister North, Montréal West, PQ, Canada, H4X 1Z3, Tel: 514-487-3242. Subscription office P.O. Box 2946, Plattsburgh, NY, USA, 12901-9863, Tel: 1-800-565-GOCD. This Canadian-based magazine is published bi-monthly by Universal Multimedia Inc.

CD-ROM Professional. 462 Danbury Road, Wilton, CT, USA, 06897, Tel: 800-248-8466/203-761-1466. Published bi-monthly by Pemberton Press Inc., *CD-ROM Professional* provides useful information on how to master and produce CD-ROM titles and related materials.

CD-ROM World Subscription and editorial offices can be reached at Meckler Corporation, 11 Ferry Lane West, Westport, CT, USA, 06880, Tel: 203-226-6967. In other countries, Meckler Corporation can be reached at Artillery House, Artillery Row, London, SW1P 1RT, UK. This is a monthly publication that covers – you guessed it – the World of CD-ROMs.

Computer Graphics World. Editorial and executive offices are located at 10 Tara Boulevard, 5th Floor, Nashua, NH, USA, 03062-2801. For subscription inquiries only, dial 918-835-3161, extension 400. Concentrating on modeling, animation and multimedia, CGW is published monthly by Penwell Publishing.

Desktop Video World. Published monthly by Techmedia Publishing, Inc., an IDG company, at 80 Elm Street, Peterborough, NH, USA, 03458, Tel: 603-9324-0100. Desktop Video World concentrates on interactive presentations, video capture and playback using desktop computers. Product reviews help you understand how to create, edit and playback audio and video.

EC&I (Electronic Composition and Imaging). Editor in Chief, *EC&I*, Youngblood Communications Corp., 2240 Midland Ave., Suite 201, Scarborough, ON, Canada, M1P 4R8, Tel: 416-299-6007. Published bimonthly, *EC&I* concentrates on the electronic composition side of multimedia. This magazine presents a cross-platform view of printing as it emerges onto the superhighway.

Inc. The Magazine for Growing Companies. Address press releases to: Editorial Manager, *Inc. Magazine*, 38 Commercial Wharf, Boston, MA, USA, 02110, Tel: 617-248-8000. Address subscriptions to: *Inc. Magazine*, P.O. Box 54129, Boulder, CO, USA, 80322-4129, Tel: 1-800-234-0999. *Inc.* highlights the successes (and failures) of medium-sized businesses. Upscale readership of corporate presidents and owner/managers. Monthly magazine that has an obvious bias toward North American service companies.

MacWorld. Published monthly by IDG Company, at 80 Elm Street, Peterborough, NH, USA, 03458, Tel: 603-9324-0100. The first issue of *MacWorld* featured then-Apple president Steve Jobs and the new 128K Macintosh. A lot has happened since then both to Apple and the Macintosh, and MacWorld has been there to cover it all.

MacWorld UK. Published by CW Communications, 99-100 Grays Inn Road, London, UK, WC1X 8UT, Tel: 01 831 9252. A popular generalist magazine dealing with Macintosh computers in the business and home/consumer markets.

MacUser. For subscriptions call MacUser, 1-800-627-2247 in the U.S. and Canada – other countries dial 303-447-9330 – or write to *MacUser* Subscriptions, P.O. Box 56986, Boulder, CO, USA, 80322-6986. Send press releases to *MacUser*, 950 Tower Lane, 18th Floor, Foster City, CA, USA, 94404. One of the literary grandparents of the computer community. This magazine is useful for in-depth articles and reviews on selected Macintosh-based products.

MacUser UK. Dennis Publishing Limited, a division of Feldon Productions, 19 Bolsover Street, London, UK, W1P 7HJ, Tel: 071-631-1433. General Macintosh magazine from the UK perspective. Published fortnightly (every two weeks).

Media Access Report. Published monthly by Media Access International Limited, 238 Davenport Road, Suite 377, Toronto, ON, Canada, M5R 1J6. This business newsletter includes in-depth coverage focusing on marketing, financial and legal matters surrounding the high-tech industry.

MIX Magazine. Published monthly by Act III Publishing located at 6400 Hollis Street #12, Emeryville, CA, USA, 94608, Tel: 510-653-3307. When sound engineers want to kick back, relax, and read a trade magazine, they read *MIX*.

Multimedia Today. Published quarterly by Redgate Communications of 660 Beachland Blvd., Vero Beach, FL, USA, 032963, Tel: 407-231-6904. The IBM-based equivalent of *The World of Macintosh Multimedia*, providing a printed directory of multimedia and related products.

Multimedia World. Published monthly by PC World Communications Inc. 501 Second Street, San Francisco, CA, USA, 94107, Tel: 800-685-3435 (in Tennessee and out of U.S. call 615-377-3322). Subscription requests can be sent to Subscriber Services, P.O. Box 5039 Brentwood, TN, USA 37024.

Network Computing. Produced by CMP Publications, Inc., 600 Community Drive, Manhasset, NY, USA, 11030. Tel: 516-512-5000. Targeted at MIS and IC professionals, *Network Computing* is read by the people who make the strategic information delivery decisions in major corporations.

NewMedia Magazine. Subscription inquiries should be sent to: *NewMedia Magazine*, P.O. Box 1771, Riverton, NJ, USA, 08077-9771, Tel: 609-764-1846. Press releases should be sent to: Editorial Department, NewMedia Magazine, 901 Mariner's Island Boulevard, Suite 365, San Mateo, CA, USA, 94404, Tel: 415-573-5170. Published monthly by HyperMedia Communications, this magazine contains news and product reviews on the new media industry. *NewMedia Magazine* is worthwhile reading to understand the features and benefits of new CD-ROM titles as well as trends within the world of multimedia.

PC Graphics & Video. Published bi-monthly by Advanstar Communications, 859 Willamette Street, Eugene, Oregon, USA, 97401-6806, Tel: 503-343-1200. This magazine deals with the PC side of the multimedia and desktop publishing industries.

PC World. Published monthly by IDG company, at 80 Elm Street, Peterborough, NH, USA, 03458, Tel: 603-9324-0100. General product reviews and other interesting information about PC-based computing.

PC Magazine. Published by Zif-Davis Publishing Company. Address press releases to 1 Park Avenue, NY, NY, USA, 10016. For subscription information contact MacWeek c/o JCI, P.O. Box 1766 Riverton, NJ, USA, 08077-7366, Tel: 609-786-8230. Good general monthly magazine about PC-based computing.

Sources

Presentations. Technology and Techniques for Better Communication. Business and editorial offices of the magazine are located at: Lakewood Publications Inc., 23410 Civic Center Way, Suite E-10, Malibu, CA, USA, 90265, Tel: 310-456-2283. For subscriptions contact: *Presentations Magazine*, P.O. Box 1142, Skokie, IL, 60076. Published monthly, *Presentations* concentrates on the business presentations market.

Publish. The Art and Technology of Electronic Publishing. Publish is published monthly by Integrated Media Inc. at 501 Second Street, San Francisco, CA, USA, 94107, Tel: 800-685-3435 (in Tennessee and outside U.S. call 615-377-3322). Subscription requests can be sent to Subscriber Services, P.O. Box 5039 Brentwood, TN, USA, 37024. This magazine is key to understanding the technology behind digital publishing and electronic books. Originally a desktop publishing magazine, *Publish* now caters to the new media mavens staking claims in the electronic publishing marketplace.

The Red Herring. The Red Herring is published monthly by Flipside Communications, Inc. at 2055 Woodside Road, Suite 240, Redwood City, CA, USA, 94061, Tel: 415-853-6853. If you have limited time, read this magazine and *Upside*. This is a highly recommended magazine focusing on the strategic marketing, finance and investment angles of the high-tech marketplace.

Upside. Published monthly by Upside Publishing Company. Address press releases to: Editorial Manager, *Upside Magazine*, 1159-B Triton Drive, Foster City, CA, USA, 94404. Tel: 415-377-0950. Subscriptions should be telephoned into: 617-745-2809. This magazine lives up to its editorial statement that it "delivers an unflinchingly honest perspective on the people and companies creating the digital revolution."

Videomaker Magazine. Published monthly by Videomaker Inc. Send press releases to P.O. Box 4591, Chico, CA, USA, 95927. For subscriptions contact P.O. Box 469026, Escondido, CA, 92046, Tel: 619-745-2809. An interesting cross between 35mm camera lens advertisements and video camera reviews.

Virtual Reality World. This bi-monthly magazine is published by Mecklermedia Corp., 11 Ferry Lane West, Westport, CN, USA, 06880, Tel: 203-226-6967. A relative new-comer chronicling this emerging area of computer technology.

Windows Magazine. Published monthly by CMP Publications, Inc., 600 Community Drive, Manhasset, NY, USA, 11030, Tel: 516-512-5000. *Windows Magazine* is another general magazine catering to the millions of Windows users.

Wired. Published monthly by Wired Ventures Ltd., 544 2nd Street, San Francisco, CA, USA, 94107-1427. Tel: 415-904-0660. *Wired* bills itself as the *Vanity Fair* of the technological elite. Fun reading cover to cover if only for its new wave insights.

The World of Macintosh Multimedia. Published quarterly by Redgate Communications (an America OnLine company), 660 Beachland Blvd., Vero Beach, FL, USA, 32963, Tel: 407-231-6904. *The World of Macintosh Multimedia* is a printed directory of over 2000 multimedia related products and is updated every three months. This is the Mac-based equivalent of *Multimedia Today.*

CONTROLLED TRADE MAGAZINES

AV Video. Published monthly by Montage Publishing, Inc., a division of Knowledge Industry Publications Inc., 701 Westchester Avenue, White Plains, NY, USA, 10604, Tel: 914-328-9157. This magazine concentrates on production and presentation technology.

CFO. The Magazine for Senior Financial Executives. Published monthly by The Economist Group, 253 Summer Street, Boston, MA, USA, 02210, Tel: 617-345-9700. This magazine covers the high-tech industry from a financial and corporate investment perspective.

Computer Pictures. For Creators and Designers of Digital Graphics, Multimedia and Prepress Production. Published bi-monthly by Montage Publishing, Inc., a division of Knowledge Industry Publications Inc., 701 Westchester Avenue, White Plains, NY, USA, 10604, Tel: 914-328-9157. Primarily a computer prepress magazine making the transition from still images to moving ones.

Computer Reseller News, a CMP Publication, 600 Community Drive, Manhasset, NY, USA, 11030, Tel: 516-512-5000. This weekly 200 (!) plus page newspaper covers all the news and rumors that are fit to print about the North American reseller industry.

Computer Retail Week. Another CMP Publication, 600 Community Drive, Manhasset, NY, USA, 11030. Tel: 516-512-5000. Covers the computer retailing side of who's buying what and why, on a week-to-week basis. This magazine focuses its attention on the consumer rather than the reseller.

Datamation. Produced by Cahners Publishing, a division of Reed Publishing, 275 Washington Street, Newton, MA, USA, 02158, Tel. 617-558-4281. Heavy duty MIS-type magazine designed for Chief Information Officers at large corporations. This magazine has been around for over 25 years, and is still going strong.

EDN, The Design Magazine of the Electronics Industry. Published by Cahners Publishing, a division of Reed Publishing, 275 Washington Street, Newton, MA, USA, 02158, Tel: 617-558-4281. Highly technical monthly magazine designed for electronics engineers.

Electronic Buyers' News. Yet another CMP Publication, 600 Community Drive, Manhasset, NY, USA, 11030, Tel: 516-512-5000. This weekly newspaper is targeted at purchasing, materials, and corporate management.

Film & Video Magazine. The Production Magazine. Published monthly by Optic Music, Inc., 8455 Beverly Blvd., Suite 508, Los Angeles, CA, USA, Tel: 213-653-8053. Hollywood producers, directors and other similar types read this one. A useful industry source for news and stories about the big screen.

Information Week. Produced by CMP Publications, Inc., 600 Community Drive, Manhasset, NY, USA, 11030. Tel: 516-512-5000. As you might have picked up from the name, *Information Week* is about information and is published weekly. This is the *Newsweek* of the information industry from a corporate viewpoint.

MacWeek. Published by Zif-Davis Publishing Company. Address press releases to 1 Park Avenue, NY, NY, USA, 10016. For subscription information contact *MacWeek* c/o JCI, P.O. Box 1766 Riverton, NJ, 08077-7366, Tel: 609-786-8230. If you are developing or marketing any Macintosh-based product or service don't miss this weekly newspaper.

Network World. An International Data Group (IDG) publication, 161 Worcester Road, Framingham, MA, USA, 01701, Tel: 508-875-6400. For over 10 years, *Network World* has been reporting weekly on the comings and goings of the computer network and connectivity industries. Read it to understand how multimedia and other new media technologies are being implemented across entire corporations.

PC Week. Published by Zif-Davis Publishing Company. Address press releases to 1 Park Avenue, NY, NY, USA, 10016. For subscription information contact *PCWeek* c/o JCI, P.O. Box 1766 Riverton, NJ, 08077-7366, Tel: 609-786-8230. If you are developing or marketing any PC-based product or service don't miss this weekly newspaper. (See *MacWeek* above.)

VARBusiness. Published monthly with additional issues in March, May, June, September, October, November by CMP Publications Inc., 600 Community Drive, Manhasset, NY, USA, 11030, Tel: 516-562-7608. This magazine is highly recommended for understanding the value-added reseller marketplace and distribution channels. Although it focuses on the American markets exclusively, it is extremely useful for understanding who is selling what to whom.

Books

Some people in the industry believe that the only useful information about the rapidly evolving market is found in magazines and journals. In fact, many books contain useful advice which retains its value over time. The books listed here are by no means an exhaustive set, but they represent some industry standards and other books that we have found useful. We have divided the books into those concentrating on business and those with a technological slant. Where possible we have included an ISBN (International Standard Business Number) to make it easier for you to find the book.

BOOKS ON BUSINESS, FINANCE, AND MARKETING

Business Plans that Win $$$. Stanley R. Rich and David E. Gumpert. NY: Harper & Row. ISBN: 0-060-91391-6. Based on the approach used at the MIT enterprise forum, this book takes you on a methodical journal through a business plan.

Creating Multimedia. Tom Badgett & Corey Sandler Inc. John Wiley & Sons. ISBN: 0-471-58928-4. Includes the CD-ROM: The IBM Ultimedia Tools Series CD. A basic multimedia primer for PC-based users and developers.

Creating Multimedia Presentations. Douglas Wolfgram, ed. Que Books. ISBN: 1-56529-667-2. This book gives you the basics on the creative side of this huge sector of the multimedia business.

Finance for Non-Financial Managers. Pierre G. Bergeron. Methuen Publications (a division of the Carswell Company Limited), Agincourt, ON, Canada. ISBN: 0-458-98800-6. Although somewhat tedious and dry, this book takes you on a detailed path through the nitty-gritty accounting elements every manager needs to know.

Getting to Yes – Negotiating Agreement without Giving In. Roger Fischer and William Ury. Harmondsworth, Middlesex, UK: Penguin Books Ltd. ISBN: 0-140-06534-2. The mediators' bible, this book was based on studies and conferences conducted at Harvard University.

Guerrilla Marketing – Secrets for Making Big Profits for Your Small Business. Jay Conrad Levinson. NY: Houghton-Mifflin. ISBN: 0-395-64496-8. It's the '90s and you need a marketing book like this one – short, to the point, and deadly against your competition if you use the author's suggestions.

Guerrilla Marketing Weapons: 100 Affordable Marketing Methods for Maximizing Profits from Your Small Business. Jay Conrad Levinson. New York: Plume, a division of Penguin Books, USA. ISBN: 0-452-26519-3. These 100 targeted weapons add potency to the guerrilla marketing attack.

The Haggler's Handbook – One Hour to Negotiating Power. Leonard Koren and Peter Goodman. NY: W.W. Norton and Co. ISBN: 0-303-02981-6. If you have to negotiate a contract or anything else, hire a lawyer and read this book.

The High Tech Marketing Companion. Edited by Dee Kiamy. Addison Wesley Publishers Limited. ISBN: 0-201-62666-7. If you read one book in this list, Dee's book should be it.

How to Work the Competition into the Ground and Have Fun Doing It. John T. Molloy. NY: Warner Books, Inc. ISBN: 0-446-38499-2. From the author of *Dress for Success*, the author takes you through 1980s-style productivity exercises. Helps you understand why Suits have ulcers by the time they are 40 years old. Analyze this book to avoid a similar fate.

Marketing Geography. Ross L. Davies. Methuen and Company. ISBN: 0-416-70700-9. Heavy-duty academic book dealing with where to put your retail store and product.

Marketing Warfare. Al Ries & Jack Trout. NY: McGraw-Hill, Inc. ISBN: 0-452-25861-8. Called a complete marketing manifesto by many marketing experts, *Marketing Warfare* contains the core marketing ideas that can make your venture successful.

Multimedia Law Handbook. Menlo Park, CA: Ladera Press. This book provides legal guidelines for developers and publishers.

The Portable MBA. Eliza G.C. Collins and Mary Anne Devanna. Toronto, Canada: John Wiley & Sons, Inc. ISBN: 0-471-61997-3. For those who can't (or won't) go to MBA school, this book gives you enough information to let you keep your head above water when dealing with Suits.

Professional Selling. Robert Anderson. Englewood Cliffs, NJ: Prentice-Hall, Inc. ISBN: 0-13-75912-3. When professional sales people go through formal training sessions this is the material they learn.

Publish Yourself on CD-ROM – Mastering CDs for Multimedia. Fabrizio Caffarelli & Deirdré Straughan. Random House Electronic Publishing. ISBN: 0-679-74297-2. A somewhat technical but very informative book dealing with how to make your own ISO 9660-, Windows-, and Macintosh-compatible CD-ROMs.

Successful Telemarketing – Opportunities and Techniques for Increasing Sales and Profits. Bob Stone and John Wyman. NTC Business Books, a division of National Textbook Company. ISBN: 0-8442-3133-9. Although dated, this book offers a good introduction to telemarketing.

Total Customer Service – The Ultimate Weapon: A Six Point Plan for Giving Your Business the Competitive Edge in the 1990s. William H. Davidow and Bro Uttal. HarperCollins Publishers. ISBN: 0-06-092009-2. A guidebook for implementing successful customer service strategies within your company.

The Virtual Corporation. Structuring and Revitalizing the Corporation for the 21st Century. NY: William Davidow & Michael Malone. Harper Business. ISBN: 0-88730-593-8. This is a good book if you work for (or if you're a vendor to) a large corporation.

What Every Manager Needs to Know about Marketing. David Freiman, editor. NY: American Management Association. ISBN: 0-8144-7666-X. Contains excerpts from the AMA Management Handbook, providing a translation form MBA-talk to English.

Books on Technology

The Apple CD-ROM Handbook. Addison-Wesley Publishers Limited. ISBN: 0-201-63230-6. Although this book contains some dated material it is a good introduction to CD-ROM production.

Apple Human Interface Guidelines. Addison-Wesley Publishers Limited. ISBN: 0-201-17753-6. An introduction to the design principles of Apple's desktop interface.

CD-I Design Handbook. Addison-Wesley Publishers Limited. ISBN: 0-201-62749-3. This book describes the Philips CD-I (Compact Disc-Interactive) design process from initial idea stage to the beginning of production.

CD-I Production Handbook. Addison-Wesley Publishers Limited. ISBN: 0-201-63230-6. Another handbook from Philips, this book takes you through the CD-I development process.

Multimedia Demystified. A Guide to the World of Multimedia from Apple Computer. Apple Computer, Inc. ISBN: 0-679-75603-5. Available through APDA Tel: 716-871-6555, and Random House Electronic Publishing Tel: 410-848-1900, ext. 3000. Good case studies of multimedia developers and some good advice about the market.

Inside Macintosh: QuickTime. Apple Technical Library published by Addison-Wesley Publishers Limited. ISBN: 0-201-62201-7. Basically for programmers writing code, this book is indispensable if you need the low-down on the bits and bytes of QuickTime.

Macintosh Multimedia Workshop. Michael Murie. Hayden Books. ISBN: 1-56830-018-2. A general (i.e., very introductory) overview of the tools used in making multimedia on Apple Macintosh computers. Includes a CD-ROM with over 400 MB of demos and samples.

Making It Macintosh. Addison-Wesley Publishers Limited. ISBN: 0-201-62626-8. This CD-ROM disc is a companion to *Apple Human Interface Guidelines.* This is an interactive guide to human/computer interface design for the Macintosh. This CD-ROM disc contains over 100 animated examples that demonstrate the correct use of Macintosh interface elements, and that help you identify and solve interface design problems.

Multimedia Computing – Case Studies from MIT Project Athena. Matthew Hodges and Russell Sasnett. Addison-Wesley Publishers Limited. ISBN: 0-201-52029-X. Useful for understanding the academic framework of multimedia computing.

QuickTime Handbook. The Complete Guide to Mac Movie Making. David Drucker & Michael Murie. Hayden Press. ISBN: 0-672-48533-8. Good overview on QuickTime in general and some issues involved in production. .

TOG on Interface. Bruce "TOG" Tognazzini. Addison-Wesley Publishers Limited. ISBN: 0-201-60842-1. Invaluable resource for multimedia developers to ensure the visual interface of their projects is both efficient and easy-to-use. Investment and other financial specialists will benefit from this book because it can help them evaluate the interface and other design principles of multimedia projects.

Video User's Handbook. The Complete Illustrated Guide to Operating and Maintaining Your Video Equipment. Peter Utz. NY: Prentice Hall Press, ISBN: 0-13-941899-7. Good introduction for video work.

BOOKS AVAILABLE ONLY THROUGH THE APPLE MULTIMEDIA PROGRAM (AMP)

Published by Apple Computer, Inc., Cupertino, CA, USA, Tel: 408-996-1010. Many of these books were sources for statistics contained within this book.

Apple Guide to Producing Localized Multimedia.
International Contact, Inc.

Apple Multimedia Training Guide. Dana De Puy Morgan

Breaking Though. Joel Nagy

CD-ROM Market Segmentation and Buyer Profile Report.
Dana De Puy Morgan.

Optical Storage Media Market Research Report. Dana De Puy Morgan

Trends in CD-ROM and Multimedia Delivery. Patty Kammerer.

The Apple Multimedia Program (AMP) is an annual fee-based program designed for multimedia title publishers, production companies, in-house developers, system integrators, and consultants. Membership in the program includes special discounts, market research reports, technical guidebooks, CD-ROMs and videos, product and service directories, special opportunities for training, marketing, and trade shows, as well as a "Members Only" bulletin board that allows you to tap into technical and marketing tips and techniques. For further information or an application call 408-974-4897.

Trade Shows and Conferences

These shows come in two broad categories based on their intended market. General trade shows like Digital World in Los Angeles, for example, allow any interested party to pay an entrance fee, wander in and explore. Closed shows – like Comdex – require attendees to hold certain job qualifications or titles. Trade shows also tend to move around from year to year, so the months and locations provided below should only be taken as a general guide.

January

Consumer Electronics Show: Las Vegas, NV, USA
Electronic Industries Association, 202-457-4900

Macworld: San Francisco, CA, USA
Mitch Hall Associates, 617-361-2001

Milia: Cannes, France
Midem Organization, France: 33-1-44-34-4444. USA: 212-689-4220. UK: 44-71-528-0086. Germany: 49-89-33-5390. Japan: 81-3-3290-3019

February

Digital Hollywood/Home Media: Beverly Hills, CA, USA
American Expositions, 212-226-4141

Macworld Tokyo: Tokyo, Japan
World Expo Corporation, 508-879-6700

Virtual Reality International: London, UK
Meckler, Ltd. US: 203-226-6967, Europe: 44-071-976-0405

March

The Business Software Solutions Conference & Software Development Conference (Previously Known As Windows OS/2 San Jose) San Jose, CA, USA. CM Ventures Inc., 415-905-2784

CeBIT Hannover: Hannover, Germany
Deutsche Messe AG

Electronic Books International: London, UK
Meckler, Ltd., US: 203-226-6967, Europe: 44-071-976-0405

Fose's CD-ROM Conference: Washington D.C., USA
National Trade Productions, Inc., 800-638-8510 or 703-683-8500

Intermedia: San Jose, CA, USA
Reed Exhibition, 203-352-8240

International QuickTime And Multimedia Conference & International Film Festival: San Francisco, CA, USA. Sumeria, 415-904-0811

National Association of Broadcasters (NAB) Show: Las Vegas, NV, USA
National Association of Broadcasters, 202-429-5409

Seybold Boston, New Prospects For Power Publishers: Boston, MA, USA
Seybold Seminars, 310-457-8500

April

AIIM Show And Conference: New York, NY, USA
Association For Information & Image Management, 301-587-8202

Electronic Entertainment Expo: Atlanta, GA, USA
Knowledge Industries Publications, 914-328-9157

Imageworld Chicago: Chicago, IL, USA
Meckler, Ltd., US: 203-226-6967, Europe: 44-071-976-0405

New Media Expo: Los Angeles, CA, USA
The Interface Group, 617-449-6600

MAY

Apple Worldwide Developer Conference: San Jose, CA, USA
Apple Computer, Inc., 408-974-4897

Comdex/Spring: Atlanta, GA or Chicago, IL, USA
The Interface Group, 617-449-6600

Computer Animation (International Festival Of Computer-Animated Films): Geneva, Switzerland
Secretariat: Cui, 24 Rue Du Général-Dufour, 1204 Genève, 41-22-705-7769

Multimedia: Oakland, CA, USA
National Educational Film & Video Festival, 510-465-6885

Multimedia: Toronto Convention Centre, Toronto, Canada
Multimedia Exposition And Forum, 416-660-2491, 800-888-7564

Virtual Reality: San Jose, CA, USA
Meckler Ltd., 800-632-5537

JUNE

AMI: New Orleans, LA, USA
Association For Multi-Image International, 813-960-1692

Computer Graphics International: Melbourne, Australia
61-3-2822463

Consumer Electronics Show – Summer: Chicago, IL, USA
Electronic Industries Association, 202-457-4900

Interactive: San Jose, CA, USA
Ziff Institute. 617-252-5187

Multimedia Conference And Exhibition: London, UK
Blenheim Group PLC, 44-81-742-2828

NECC (National Education Computer Conference): Boston, MA, USA
NECC, 503-346-4414

Seybold Digital World Conference: Los Angeles, CA, USA
Seybold Seminars, 310-457-8500

Technology & Issues: Yosemite, CA, USA
Sumeria, 415-904-0811

Viscomm: San Francisco, CA, USA
United Digital Artists, 212-777-7200

JULY

ACM Siggraph: various locations, USA
Siggraph Conference Management, 312-644-6610

AUGUST

Macworld: Boston, MA, USA
Mitch Hall Associates, 617-361-2001

Salt Conference/Interactive Multimedia: Washington, D.C., USA
Society For Applied Learning, 800-457-6812

SEPTEMBER

Agenda: Scottsdale, AZ, USA
Infoworld Editorial Events, 415-312-0545

Electronic Books New York: New York, NY, USA
Meckler, Ltd. 800-632-5537

Electronic Book Fair: San Francisco, CA, USA
Sumeria, 415-904-0811

Imageworld New York: New York, NY, USA
Knowledge Industry Publications, 800-800-5474

Macromedia International Developers Conference: San Francisco, CA, USA. Reed Exhibition Companies, 203-352-8296

Macworld Expo Germany: Frankfurt/Berlin, Germany
49-61-51-26121

Multimedia Expo/Digital Video: San Francisco, CA, USA
American Expositions, 212-226-4141

Seybold San Francisco: San Francisco, CA, USA
Seybold Seminars, 310-457-8500

Windows Solutions Conference & Exhibition: San Francisco, CA, USA
Seybold Seminars, 310-457-8500

OCTOBER

CD-ROM Expo: Boston, MA, USA
Mitch Hall Associates, 617-361-2001

Macworld Expo Canada: Toronto, Ontario
Mitch Hall Associates, 617-361-2001

Multimedia Expo: San Jose Convention Center, CA, USA
American Expositions Inc., 212-226-4141

Smart Media: New York, NY, USA
Knowledge Industry Publications, 800-800-5474

Time Europe/CD-ROM Europe: Wembley Complex, London, UK
Lowndes Exhibition Organizers Ltd., 44-0-733-394-304

November

Comdex/Fall: Las Vegas, NV, USA
The Interface Group, 617-449-6600

European Multimedia and CD-ROM Conference:
Wiesbaden, Germany, 49-211-55-62-81

New York Virtual Reality Expo: New York, NY, USA
Meckler, Ltd., 800-632-5537

Nicograph: Tokyo, Japan
Nippon Computer Graphics Association, 81-3-3233-3475

December

Imageworld West: San Jose, CA, USA
Knowledge Industry Publications, 800-800-5474

INDEX

Accel Partners, 177
accountant, 30, 66-67, 71, 74, 77-78, 106, 168
accumulated depreciation, 70
acid test, 74
Adobe, 54, 120, 126
    Adobe Systems, 120
advances, 19, 70, 83
adventure game, 142
advertising, 20, 27, 44, 46-47, 67-68, 80-82, 84, 86, 91, 103, 107, 135, 141, 145, 152-154, 164, 166
affiliate label, 26, 82-84, 136
Afga, 126
anchor product, 97
animation, 6, 13-14, 27, 49, 165, 189
animators, 8, 13-14, 43
annual report, 129
Apple Computer, 28, 120, 130, 137, 169, 200, 202
approved vendors list, 113
archiving, 121-122
Aris Entertainment, 175
artists, 8, 16, 119, 163
Asia CD Ltd., 173
Asset Management, 178
assets, 36, 48, 67, 69-71, 73-75, 78, 161
Assistant Secretary and Commissioner, 180
    of Patents & Trademarks, 180
AT&T, 99-100, 198
    AT&T Ventures, 178
Atari, 43
audio specialists, 8, 14
Australian MacWorld, 188
AV Video, 194

Baker & Taylor Software, 170, 175
balance sheet, 65-66, 69-71, 73
Battery Ventures, 178
Bessemer Venture Partners, 178
Blockbuster Entertainment Co., 175
books, 22, 28-29, 42, 78, 115, 120, 138, 141, 144-145, 161, 169, 176, 193, 197-202
    business, finance, 197
    marketing, 6-7, 10, 12, 19, 26, 39, 43, 47, 84, 93, 140-141, 163, 197, 202
    technology, 200
break-even analysis, 41
Brøderbund, 26, 115, 136, 175
    Brøderbund Software, Inc., 136, 175
budget analysis, 64
bundle, 54, 96-98, 107
    bundle price, 54
    bundling, 19, 57, 89, 94, 96-99, 107, 113
    bundling tradeoffs, 98
Burr, Egan, Deleage, 178
Business Research Group, 124
Business Week, 189

business cycle, 33
business plan, 9-11, 30-32, 34-41, 45, 49, 93, 104, 157, 159, 161, 197
business planning, 3, 30-31, 33, 35, 37, 39, 41, 43
business presentations, 21, 50-51, 124-127, 130, 132, 155, 175, 193

Cambrix Publishing, 175
Canaan Partners, 178
capital account, 69
cartographic products, 143
cash infusion milestones, 34
cash requirements, 34-35
Catena Corp., Packaged Software, 174
    Publishing Center, 174
CBT, 7, 126
CD-Interactive, 140
CD-R, 132
    CD-Recordable, 132
CD-ROM Multimedia Magazine, 189
CD-ROM Professional, 189
CD-ROM World, 189
CFO, 194
checkout-friendly packaging, 94
Claris Clear Choice, 137, 175
coders, 8, 17
Comdex, 152, 203
competition, 29, 31, 35, 37, 53, 91, 94, 96, 130, 135, 152-153, 158, 198
compression, 14, 21
Compton's, 26, 137, 140, 142, 152, 175
    Compton's New Media, 26, 137, 140, 175
Computer Graphics World, 189
Computer Pictures, 195
Computer Reseller News, 195
Computer Retail Week, 195
computer dealers, 52
computer-based training, 7, 101, 126
Computers Unlimited, 172
consignment, 88, 94
consumer publishing, 136
content experts, 8, 15
controlled trade magazines, 194
Copyright and Industrial Design Branch, 181
copyright, 3, 10-11, 70, 120, 181
Coral Group, 178
Corel Systems, 137, 176
cost center, 102
cost of goods sold, 67-68, 94, 166
Creative Multimedia Corporation, 176
credit card authorization, 87
cross-promotional event, 47

D&H Distributing, 170
Datamation, 195
Dataquest, 151, 155, 186
debt financing, 9
debt to equity, 74
demographic profile, 35
depreciation method, 77
Desktop Video World, 190
desktop publishing packages, 97
development costs, 143
development cycle, 49, 163
development time, 3, 33
digitally manipulated images, 49
digitization, 14
dimensionality, 86
direct-to-the-customer advertising, 80
director, 7-9, 13, 15-16, 38, 146, 162
Discis, 26, 28, 115, 138, 176
Disney, 48, 135, 138, 176
distribution, 3, 9-10, 12, 14, 28, 31, 34, 39, 41, 50, 57-60, 80-99, 107, 113, 136-137, 139, 157, 162-163, 170, 172, 197
    distribution model, 39
Draper Associates, 179
duplication, 51, 82, 84

e-mail, 122, 130
Eastman Kodak, 120
Edgar Allen Poe, 115
editor, 55, 98, 146-147, 149, 154, 190, 200
EDN, The Design Magazine of the Electronics Industry, 195
education sales cycle, 110
educational pricing, 109
Educorp, 139, 170, 176
Electronic Arts, 26, 176
Electronic Buyers' News, 195
electronic press releases, 150
EMJ, 171
En Passant, 22-23, 126
equity, 9, 69-70, 74-75, 162
    equity financing, 9
Euro-CD, 139, 172, 176
executive producer, 146
executive summary, 35, 161
existing retail channel, 98
Expanded Book Toolkit, 141

Film & Video Magazine, 196
financial projections, 36
financial status, 31
financing leverage, 11
Focal Point Computer, Inc., 174
freelancers, 146, 154
Frontline Distribution, 172
fulfillment, 61, 84-86, 89-91, 107
    fulfillment companies, 90

future viability, 34
FWB Inc., 120

GEM Distribution Company, 172
general circulation magazines, 188
Generally Accepted Accounting
    Principles (GAAP), 71
goodwill, 69-70
graphic designers, 16, 43
Grolier Electronic Publishing, 140, 176

home video rental model, 6

illustrators, 16
image scanning, 16
Inc. The Magazine for Growing Companies, 190
income statement, 66-69, 71, 73
incorporate, 21, 27, 42, 48, 65, 114-115, 118, 122, 142, 144, 153
Industrial Revolution, 118
infomercials, 22, 46, 164
Information Week, 196
Ingram, 91, 93, 169, 171
inlay cards, 87
Institutional Venture Partners, 179
instructional curricula, 113
Inteco Corporation, 134, 187
Intel, 123, 132
    Intel's ProShare, 123
interactivity, 6, 123
interface designers, 8, 17
investors, 2, 8, 11-13, 31-32, 34-35, 37-41, 64-65, 71- 72, 74-78, 93, 189
investors and venture capitalists, 11

jewel case, 94
just-in-time training, 24, 126, 130

Kenfill Distribution, 170
kiosks, 20-21, 24, 27, 41-42, 60-62, 126, 132, 164
Kleiner, Perkins, Caulfield & Buyers, 179

liabilities, 69-71, 73, 75
licensing, 14, 19, 78, 135, 137, 141, 163, 168, 181
liquid, 71
listed corporations, 65
localization, 49, 101, 139
locational plan, 40-41, 165
Lotus Development, 91

Index

Macromedia, 120
MacUser, 191
   MacUser UK, 191
MacWeek, 192, 196
MacWorld, 152-153, 188, 190, 203
   MacWorld UK, 190
magazines and journals, 188, 197
Management Information Services, 123
management team, 36, 38, 42, 162
market localization, 101
market performance, 32
market research, 10, 49, 54, 93, 104, 164, 186, 202
marketing bandwidth, 52, 84
marketing leverage, 48, 106
marketing manager, 7, 94, 97
marketing plan, 39, 41, 49-50, 56, 157, 164
marketing push, 84
marketing requirements documents (MRDs), 44
Matrix Partners, 179
Mayfield Fund, 179
Media Access Report, 96, 191
Media Exchange, 173
Media Television, 146
media, 8, 12, 17, 26, 43, 50, 55, 96, 119-120, 135, 137, 140, 142, 145-146, 151, 173, 175, 177, 186, 189, 191-193, 196, 202-20
Menlo Ventures, 179
Merisel, 91, 93, 170-171, 17
   Merisel Australia, 173
   Merisel Canada, 171
Merrill, Pickard, Anderson & Eyre, 179
Microsoft, 2, 48, 110, 120, 132, 142, 149
milestone invoicing, 33
Mitch Hall and Associates, 153
MIX Magazine, 191
Mohr, Davidow Ventures, 180
movie model, 6-7
Multimedia Food Chain, 3, 7-9, 11, 13, 15, 17, 38
Multimedia Today, 158, 191, 194
Multimedia World, 11, 39, 43, 61-62, 79, 191
multimedia authoring solutions, 97
music industry model, 6

National Geographic Society, 138
Network Computing, 192
Network World, 196
New Media Centers, 17, 119
NewMedia Magazine, 192
news release, 149, 160
Nintendo, 23, 26, 43, 140
Northern Telecom, 24, 123
   Northern Telecom's Visit, 123
Novell, 132

objectives, 10, 34, 50-53, 157
OEM (original equipment manufacturer), 98
   OEM product, 99
Oki Software, Packaged Software Division, 174

One Stop Micro, 171
one-off machines, 150
operating performance, 32
opportunity cost, 86
organizational chart, 127
OST Chart, 50-51
out-of-pocket expenses, 33
outsourcing, 3, 86
overall performance, 32
ownership structure, 37, 162

P&L, 66, 173
packaging, 19, 44-45, 81-86, 88, 94, 98-99, 139
Paramount, 135, 140
Parent Teacher Association, 111
past performance, 32, 38
patents, 36, 70, 165, 180
PC Graphics & Video, 192
PC Magazine, 192
PC Week, 196
PC World, 191-192
Philips, 140, 177, 200
   Philips Interactive Media of America, 140, 177
photographers, 16
portfolio footage, 14
PR firms, 151-152
Prentice Hall, 120, 202
present performance, 32
Presentations, 21, 27, 46, 50-52, 101, 118, 121, 124-127, 129-130, 132, 155, 175, 190, 193, 197
press, 3, 8, 12, 44-45, 47, 50, 52, 55, 94, 145-154, 188-193, 196, 199, 201-202
   press and media relations, 12, 55
   press conference, 147
   press kits, 50, 149
   press releases, 45, 47, 55, 148, 150-151, 154, 188, 190-193, 196
Principal Distribution Ltd., 172
producer, 6-10, 12-13, 38, 95-96, 103, 146, 149, 162-163
product marketing, 53, 85, 199
product submission kit, 139
profit and loss (P&L) statement, 66
program requirements documents (PRDs), 44
project management skills, 9, 13
project management software, 35, 38, 40
project manager, 7, 38, 43
project plan, 35, 38, 163
projected income statement, 69
Publish, 26, 81-82, 138, 154, 193, 199
publisher, 7, 26, 81-84, 136-141, 146, 154, 170, 175-177
publishing model, 6-7

Index

QED, 108, 113-115, 117, 188
    Quality Education Data, 108, 188

racking, 60, 94, 137
Radius, 54, 124
recognition factor, 96, 100, 103
recordable CD-ROM, 53
Red Herring, 96, 193
    The Red Herring, 193
Regis McKenna, 151
Registrar of Trade-marks, 180
registration cards, 99
replication, 85, 92, 98
reporters, 145-148, 150, 154
research and development plan, 40, 164
resource costing, 35
retail packaging, 86, 94, 99
retained earnings, 66, 70-73
review editors, 55
royalties, 83

sales and marketing consultants, 10
salvage value, 77
school boards, 108, 111, 114, 117-118
search engine, 143
security deposit, 87
self-publishing, 26, 81-84, 87
Sequoia Capital, 180
shop-lifting, 87
shrink-wrapping, 94
shrinkage, 87-88
Siemens, 123
Sigma Partners, 180
social science, 118
software maintenance model, 6-7
solutions marketing, 53-55, 108-109, 111, 113, 115, 117, 119, 121, 123, 125, 127, 129, 131, 133-135, 137, 139, 141, 143
Sonic the Hedgehog, 42
Sony Corporation, 120, 140
    Sony Electronic Publishing, 26, 83
sound synchronization, 14
spiffs, 53
spoilage, 87
sports titles, 144
staff and locational plan, 40, 165
still photographs, 123, 142, 146
storyboarding, 14, 33, 39, 163
strategies, 10, 32, 50, 52-53, 92, 107, 129, 157, 199
Summit Partners, 180
SuperMac, 120
Swire Transtech Ltd., 174

tactics, 10, 50, 52-53, 157
tax inspectors, 78
taxes, 67, 70, 78, 166
teaser, 95, 103
Tech Data, 91, 170

Tech Pacific, 173
technology lawyer, 10-11
Texas, 92, 117
The Red Herring, 193
The Tell Tale Heart, 115
The Voyager Company, 28, 83, 141, 144, 177
The World of Macintosh Multimedia, 191, 194
Time Warner, 140, 177
    Time Warner Interactive, 140, 177
time lines, 34
trademark, 3, 10-11, 180
Truevision, 124
TWI, 140

Universal Product Code, 94
Upside, 193

VARBusiness, 197
venture capital, 38, 95
    venture capitalists, 2, 9, 11, 31, 37-38, 79, 93, 169, 177
vertical market, 97
Video on Demand, 127
video clips, 11, 15, 18, 139
video editing solutions, 97
video game model, 6
video specialists, 8, 14
Videomaker Magazine, 193
Virtual Reality World, 194
VOD, 127
Voyager Company, 28, 83, 141, 144, 177

Wayzata Technology, 141, 177
wholesale price, 82, 98
Windows Magazine, 194
Windows on Science, 117
wire services, 147
Wired, 127, 194
World of Macintosh Multimedia, 100, 191, 194
worst case scenarios, 41
writers, 8, 15, 43, 47, 55, 100, 147, 150, 153, 163

Xiphias, 177